Angels Sing
in me

Also by James Dillet Freeman

Books

Be!
A Case for Believing
The Case for Optimism
The Case for Reincarnation
Happiness Can Be a Habit
The Hilltop Heart: Reflections of a Practical Mystic
Look With Eyes of Love
Love Is Strong as Death: Moving Through Grief
Love, Loved, Loving!
Of Time and Eternity
Once Upon a Christmas
Prayer: The Master Key
The Story of Unity
What God Is Like

Audiocassettes

Angels Sing in Me: The Best of James Dillet Freeman
Freeman's Christmas Stories

Angels Sing in me

The James Dillet Freeman Memorial Book

Compiled and Edited by Michael A. Maday and Philip White

unity® HOUSE

Unity Village, Missouri

First Edition 2004
Second Printing 2005

For information on all Unity publications go to *www.unityonline.org* or call Customer Service: 1-800-669-0282.

The publisher wishes to acknowledge the copy services of Kay Thomure, Marlene Barry, Jenny Leckbee, and Cassie Thompson; the creative and production services of Lisa Pruyn, Terry Newell, Linda Castle, Joann Simcoe, Lisa Hurst, and Susan Anderson; and the marketing efforts of Kim West, Wendy Rumsey, Adrianne Ford, and Sharon Sartin.

All Bible verses are in NRSV unless otherwise noted.

Cover and interior design by Jenny Hahn Neely

Photographs courtesy of Unity Archives and Virginia Love

Library of Congress Control Number: 2003117001

ISBN 0-87159-295-9

Canada BN 13252 9033 RT

I am God's song.
Listen for me.
You are God's song.
Listen.

—James Dillet Freeman

Table of Contents

Introduction by Michael A. Maday 1

I. Writing 15
To Begin 16
Angels Sing in Me 17
Poetry Is Song 18
The Way of the Heart.............. 21

II. Purpose 25
I'm a Seeker........................... 26
Lord, Help Me to Help People
   Not to Hurt So Much 27
The Fruit of God................... 28
A Minister 29
Footprints 30
Life's Child 31

III. Meaning 33
Perfection's Imminence........... 33
A World Alive 34
Be! 36
How Can I Know? 41
We Have to Live Here and Now .. 46
Upon This Flame 47

IV. God 49
What God Is Like................... 49
Because He Is Love 50
Presence 52
Love's Purple Patches.............. 53
Of Gnat's Wings 54
"Whom My Soul Loveth" 55
Size........................... 57

V. Life 59
A Beauty on the Land 59
I Am God's Song 60

The World Is Not What the
   World Seems 61
What Is a Tree?....................... 62
A Jigsaw Puzzle 64
Life Is Change 65
Change 66
And Not a Sound Was Heard ...67
If You Reach 68
A Fish Not Even Gold.............69
To Thine Own Self 71
Rivers Hardly Ever 72
Live Young! 73
And Beauty Too!....................... 79
My Heart Makes Its Own
   Weather........................... 80
The Cherry Tree 81

VI. Love 83
Wisdom........................... 83
When We Look With Eyes
   of Love 84
Love's Omnipotence 85
She Let's Us Love Her.............. 86
The Heart Will Find Its Own ...88
I the Human Being Come With
   My Human Heart 92
What Hand Did You Expect
   Him to Use? 94
Blessing for a Marriage............96
A Praise of Sex and Love.........98

VII. Grief........................... 101
I Am There........................... 102
This Is My Gift....................... 104
Still the Glory Is Not Gone 105
A Step Back Toward Life 106

These Poems Are the Tears
    I Kept............................ 116
Anything Less Than
    Utter Trust 117
Love's Rose 119
Another Dawn 120
Snow-Flowers..................... 123
The Journey of Today 124
Sunrise................................. 125

VIII. Faith 127

Transformation 127
The Original Look 128
The Pollyanna..................... 133
March Weed 140
Oh, Yes, for You! 141
Invisibles............................. 142
"Help Thou Mine Unbelief" ..143
Mountains Affirm 148
As Still as Snow................... 149
Crocus 150
Grace................................... 151

IX. Prayer............................ 153

Homeward 153
A Wind and a Tide.............. 154
The Way of Attunement 156
Not By Might 158
Revelation 159
Fragile Things..................... 160
How Did You Turn It Off?.... 161
The Master Sat Silent.......... 162
A Further Digression on
    Truths 164
Mind's Millpond................. 166
Prayer Is Life....................... 167
Nothing Can Be Possessed... 172
Not for Forever 174

X. Jesus............................... 177

O Lord, Whose Very Name
    Is Love 177
The One We All Might Be.... 178

There Was Once a Man
    of Love 183

XI. Humankind................. 189

If Thoughts Had Shapes.......189
Immortal Journey................190
What Are We? 200
A Conversation With a
    Mayfly 206

XII. Growth 215

God Sees That We Are
    Growing..........................215
The Hilltop Heart................216
I've Come Up to Here..........217
One Step More 219
One of My Most Vivid
    Memories 220
The Stone the Builders
    Rejected..........................221
A Handful of Earth..............222
Corn...................................223
Your Unknown World..........224
To Soar 230
Although the Crowd 231
Aim 232
Of Freedom and Fences.......233

XIII. Christmas 239

If Every Day Were
    Christmas 239
Christmas: A Celebration of
    Imagination 240
Angel With a Broken Wing..254

XIV. Eternity 283

The Traveler 284
What Lies Beyond? 285
Homecoming.......................286
There Is a City....................288
If the Slayer Thinks He Slays..289
Sailor 290
I Journey On 291

Introduction

By Michael A. Maday

J im has put on invisibility.
It has dawned on me throughout this project what sport Jim Freeman must be having, freed up from this mortal coil. I imagine that he is frolicking with the angels and making a few suggestions as to how they might wish to influence things here on our planet. I certainly have invited his spirit to be in and throughout this memorial book.

1

introduction

Jim's famous poem "The Traveler" perhaps says it best:

He has put on invisibility.
Dear Lord, I cannot see—
but this I know, although the road ascends
and passes from my sight,
that there will be no night;
that You will take him gently by the hand
and lead him on
along the road of life that never ends,
and he will find it is not death but dawn.
I do not doubt that You are there as here,
and You will hold him dear.

Our life did not begin with birth.
It is not of the Earth;
and this that we call death, it is no more
than the opening and closing of a door—
and in Your house how many rooms must be
beyond this one where we rest momently.

Dear Lord, I thank You for the faith that frees,
the love that knows it cannot lose its own;
the love that, looking through the shadows, sees
that You and he and I are ever one!

So "looking through the shadows," I can see that the presence of James Dillet Freeman definitely lives on. He lives on in the lives of all of us who remember him, he lives on in the powerful prayer work done by the Silent Unity prayer ministry that he served as both worker and director for so many years, and he lives on most emphatically in his writings. It is, of course, in Jim's poetry and prose that he is most with us still.

Within this book, you will read selections of Jim's writing that we have compiled with the intention of remembering him at his best and representing his wide spectrum of ideas. I will begin by telling you a little about Jim's life, including my first encounters with him, and by sharing with you Jim's own words about his background.

It was at a Youth of Unity retreat near Ann Arbor, Michigan, that I was attending as a fledgling sponsor in the spring of 1975 when I first met James Dillet Freeman. By then he was quite famous, and his legendary gifts as a storyteller and poet were in full evidence that weekend. He gave me my first real experience of Unity as a transformative teaching, and I can hardly downplay its impact on my life. Jim was ablaze with his whimsical power, that special capacity he had of talking simply and evoking basic human emotions about ideas that were at once grand and idealistic and immediately important.

My next meeting with Jim came a little over a year later during my first visit to the world headquarters of Unity here at Unity Village. It was my first international Youth of Unity conference, and I was most impressed with the quality of both the teen leaders and staff and with the world-class beauty of the grounds. I had gone to the Peace

Chapel to meditate and emerged forty minutes later with my eyes aglow. But I also was attired in the uniform of the day, cutoff jeans and T-shirt, and my hair was long and a bit unkempt. As I walked out of the Chapel, I walked right into Jim Freeman. He was wearing sunglasses in the bright sunlight, and he stared at me and demanded to know who I was and what I was doing. As I managed my answer and as he considered it, I realized that Jim was not at all pleased. Finally, satisfied that my reason was legitimate, he let me go to ponder my experience.

Here was another side to James Dillet Freeman—the man who had seen the darker side of life and so was sometimes suspicious and even cynical when there was evidence, however fleeting, justifying it. He let me go, of course, for I had done nothing wrong except perhaps bend an informal dress code for youth sponsors. But he also gave me insight into the man behind the poetry and the stories.

I think since this book pays tribute to the man that we should know what kind of man he really was, beyond his public persona. I got to spend time with Jim again late in his life as his editor, as we worked together on his essay in

introduction

New Thought for a New Millennium and then on his compilation of poetry, *Love Is Strong as Death*, which he considered his very best work. I urged him to write an autobiography. He told me he worried about people learning how dark his early life really was, and I remember telling him that knowing that would just help us appreciate more the man he became. I am now proceeding on that assumption.

We don't really know a lot about him. We know he was born in Wilmington, Delaware, on March 20, 1912, and he made his transition on April 9, 2003. Just a few weeks earlier on his 91st birthday, the mayor of Lee's Summit, on behalf of the city council, declared March 20, 2003, as James Dillet Freeman Day to honor the man who always wanted "to help people not to hurt so much."

In 1922 Jim's mother moved him and his sister fifteen hundred miles to the Kansas City area. This represented a complete break in his life, and it included removing Jim's grandfather as an influence from his life. Jim commented on this:

"There are a number of people I would like very much to meet again. Let me talk for a moment about just one of these who was very important to me—my grandfather—and let's try to imagine what a reunion between us in the next life would be like …. He was very dear to me when I was a little boy. We never saw each other after I was ten, because my mother ran away and took me with her.…

"From bits of information my mother has let drop through the years, I think my grandfather was a tyrant with his family. I remember my lovely little grandmother almost as a shadow, and I think that's all she'd been in his presence. He'd lost all his sons—four of them—to childhood diseases, so he'd tried to make my mother into a boy. But my mother was as smart and strong-willed as he was.…

"Oh, my grandfather was a tyrant with me too, but if I resented him, I loved him so much I didn't let myself know I resented him. He had me walking before I should have, but it wasn't enough to have me tottering around on my feet when I should have still been crawling on hands and knees.

4

Pete Rhea, Billie Freeman's son.

To make sure I'd grow up to be the macho boy he wanted, he had me lugging a Civil War cannonball. A history of the Civil War, full of bloody battle pictures, was one of the first books I read. My grandfather had been a boy in the Civil War. He'd lost eight uncles in it ....

"My grandfather was an unusually strong man physically and was also a man of strong opinions and emotions. Once, a barber gave me a crew cut in November. When my grandfather saw me, he loaded his gun and started out toward the barbershop. A barber stupid enough to cut all the hair off a boy in the winter should not be allowed to do it to another one, he thought. Fortunately, my grandmother was able to call and warn the barber to get out of the shop before my grandfather got there.

"My grandfather had been raised on a farm and probably had had very little education, but he knew the value of one. He made me learn the alphabet before I could talk. He was ingenious. He would speak the letter, and I would have to point it out on a chart.

"He taught me to read and write when I was three, and the books he taught me to read were the Bible and the *Red Fairy Book*. I can't recommend them as teaching aids for little children. They both left me scared white. The *Red Fairy Book* was full of pictures of ogres and giants and trolls and witches, usually in the act of dispatching helpless human beings. My grandfather not only believed in witches, he'd known a few, he'd even shot at one or two, but he hadn't had a silver bullet in his gun, and you have to have a silver bullet to shoot a witch. You can see why I slept with a rubber dagger and a hammer under my pillow. He had me read books about the Norse gods too, and naturally Thor was my hero. He was the giant killer, and I think there were a few giants in my childhood I would have liked to use his hammer on.

"Oh, he taught me to read poetry too. I was brought up on Edgar Allan Poe. He's almost as scary as the Bible and the *Red Fairy Book*. My grandfather lured me into memorizing Poe's poems. Then he'd give me a penny to recite them for his friends.

"I'm left-handed, but because he wasn't going to have a left-handed grandson, I write with my right hand—illegibly, of course.

"Although he was short, he

introduction

was immensely strong and in his youth had been a rough-and-tumble fighter. He taught me to fight—I was never any good—and to swear like a trooper—I've been too good at that. He was a hunter and a championship trapshooter. By the time I was six, he had me out dragging a gun through the snow after him. I still have his old shotgun; he left it to me.

"I would have done anything for him. I loved him. I adored him. And I'd like to think I'll meet him again. But am I going to be a little boy of, say, eight or nine? Is he going to be a man of sixty or seventy, or whatever he was?"

Jim Freeman read some of his early poetry for Charles and Myrtle Fillmore, cofounders of the Unity movement, and they liked it and him enough to hire him for a summer job in 1929. He started working fulltime as a letter writer for Silent Unity in 1933. Between the ages of 21 and 31, Jim's life changed radically from his early youth as he

Unity's early days at 9th and Tracy in Kansas City.

gradually accepted and learned to respect the Unity people and their more expanded viewpoints. Then in 1943 he had a revelation, the specifics of which we do not know. But Jim described it:

"At thirty-one I had a spiritual experience—an intense and passionate illumination—that made such an impression, such a change in me, that I've told people that was my true birth. I was reborn at that time, through that experience. I was an entirely different person, seeing life from an entirely different viewpoint and trying to live it in an entirely different way. The thing that shows most clearly how I changed is my writing. It wasn't at all like the writing I'd done before. From then on I was James Dillet Freeman, writing the poetry and prose I have written ever since, the writing I am writing now."

Although Jim doesn't say this anywhere, I suspect that was when he dropped the 'd' that was origi-

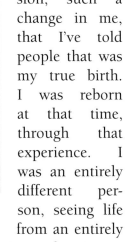

nally in his last name, and Freedman became Freeman.

"When I was thirty-five, I lost my first wife, and again I had to form all kinds of new friends and new associations.

"At fifty-five I began to travel and to talk for Unity. For twenty years before that I wouldn't talk for Unity. I never went out of Jackson County, Missouri. My wife and I stayed home and worked in our garden. I'd never been on a plane. Since then I've been in more planes than cars.... In a recent year I made fifteen trips around the United States and to foreign countries. Again, it's been a different life from the life I had twenty years ago. Then I couldn't have imagined living the life I'm living now.

"Now I'm in my seventies, and I have retired from more than fifty years' employment at Unity School, and that is making a difference again. I don't know yet what retirement will do for me.... I've lived all these different lives in one lifetime. The life that occurred to me before I was ten had almost no seeable connection with the life lived after that. My life after I was thirty-one—after I had that spiritual experience—was not in any way like the life I'd lived before, because the man who was living it was not the same man."

These words were spoken by Jim in 1984, after he had retired as first vice president of Unity School of Christianity. Before that he had been director of the ministerial program, director of spiritual research, and director of Silent Unity. His contributions to the Unity movement during this period—and since—have been immeasurable and invaluable.

Jim graduated from the University of Missouri with honors in English in 1932 and by that time had had some of his poems published nationally. Jim loved and married three women—the one he mentions above, Katherine, and then Billie, both of whom he lost to illnesses, and then Virginia who survives him. All of this, and much more, of course, is the measure of the man and the poet.

Storyteller, spokesman, lecturer—but most of all Jim Freeman was a writer and even then, mostly a poet. Even his prose often feels like poetry; something you will discover for yourself in the pages ahead.

Jim once told me that all his life he wanted to be a poet. Before he went to school, his grandfather taught him to love poetry, because he liked the poetry of Edgar Allan

7

Bill Rose, one of Jim's best friends.

introduction

Poe. Before he went to school, when he was about five, his grandfather had him memorize "Annabelle Lee." He would give Jim a penny if he would recite it to friends of his. He wanted Jim to learn "The Raven" too, but it is much longer. Jim asked, "How much will you give me if I learn that one and recite it?" He said, 'A penny.' Jim thought he was trying to teach him that poetry doesn't pay very well.

And Jim evidently learned to develop a generous sense of humor as well! No doubt Jim's grandfather gave him great depths to plumb and discover much material to wrestle the angels with! He provided fertile ground for a future poet.

So we can see that Jim's grandfather played a major role in uncovering and shaping Jim's passion in life—writing poetry—and perhaps unwittingly gave Jim much to process and overcome. Certainly as we look at the body of James Dillet Freeman's work, we see a number of themes explored again and again. We see the themes of love, of the passionate life, of faith and listening to and speaking with God, of prayers and angels, of letting go, of his deep love for Christmas, and of starting over.

Of course, many of these themes, and others, weave into one another and form the tapestry of Jim's literary work. If you've ever had the pleasure of listening to Jim speak, you know how he loved his tangents. Some of them made you forget where he was going. Sometimes they seemed to make him forget. Fortunately, his marvelous sense of humor and his storytelling magic made you not care.

A book, though, is a little different. Here we have tried to carve out some basic themes and place poetry and prose within those categories to give a taste of Freeman's literary flavors. Our fondest wish is that this book will leave you hungry for more.

I wish to acknowledge the immense help of Phil White, my friend and colleague of many years. Phil was one of Jim Freeman's closest friends, and the two met almost weekly for lunch during the last ten years of Jim's life. Phil was also the editor of *Unity Magazine* and Jim's famous "Life Is a Wonder" column. An ordained Unity minister with a master of divinity degree, Phil also has served as director of education for Unity School and dean of education for Unity's ministerial and continuing education programs.

Phil and I have together compiled the collection of prose and poetry you will soon be reading. We tried to find the best of Jim's work and perhaps that translates simply into what we liked the best. No doubt we left things out that should have been included. After all, Jim was a meticulous writer who often pointed out that if he could have said it better, he would have. However, we had to choose, and we tried to do so judiciously. The reader can at least be comforted by knowing that the selection process was done with much love.

I also want to acknowledge the help of Roxanne Ivey, also a personal friend of Jim's in his final years, who provided me her enthusiasm and love for this project early in its conception and who supplied suggestions for selection and layout. Roxanne is a poet herself, and her love for Jim Freeman's work is unparalleled in my experience.

Shortly after learning of her mentor's passing, Roxanne wrote:

"I knew the words long before I knew the man. I had even memorized some of his poetry and certain lines from his books so that I could have them with me always. It was their beauty that initially captured me—the melody they sang, the rhythm that danced across the page. But what would forever hold me were the visions that unveiled themselves so innocently with the trust and sincerity that mark all lasting power.

"Despite being raised in a world of lies and loathing, this man chose to express from a consciousness of love, every word rooted in Truth. I felt the stability of each sentiment; I could wrap myself around every thought like I would a tree and hug the hope that was offered there. Although I had been moved by many authors before and had been inspired to write a fair amount myself, I still perceived language as a mediocre means to a necessary end. But in his writing, I experienced something more, something that transcended emotion and thought. There was a meaning greater than the words themselves, a wisdom so expansive that it couldn't be contained by the letters alone but flowed through the spaces of white as well. Once lifted by this sea, I saw that writing was a form of worship, a way of service. With this realization came the undeniable directive that I must meet this poet and follow his path.

"What I found was a man too humble to advise another writer, yet too bold to deny his calling, a calling to serve humanity. Though his words are read daily around the world, uplifting hearts and enlightening minds, though they have been carried to and left on the Moon, which casts her gaze upon us night after night, he still laments. I should have been a politician, he says. Then I could have really made a difference in people's lives. He doesn't know what he has done. He has proven the power of poetry."

Perhaps Jim does know now. In any event, his impact has been massive. Two of his poems have indeed been taken and left on the Moon, something no other human poet can claim. In 1969 Apollo 11 pilot Edwin "Buzz" Aldrin, Jr. carried Freeman's "Prayer for Protection" with him as he made his historic moonwalk. Jim had written it during World War II shortly after the Japanese had bombed Pearl Harbor.

The light of God surrounds me;
The love of God enfolds me;
The power of God protects me;
The presence of God watches
over me.
Wherever I am, God is.

This poem is circulated and printed, translated and distributed in many languages around the world, usually without the author's name attached. Many people don't even know it comes from Unity let alone James Dillet Freeman. Jim really didn't care about that either since he wrote and saw it purely as a blessing for people in need, and that pretty much includes all of us.

A microfilm copy of Jim's poem "I Am There" was left on the Moon in 1971 by Apollo 15 astronaut James B. Irwin. Jim wrote this poem just as his first wife Katherine was dying. The incredible story of how it came to be formed, along with the poem itself, can be found later in this collection.

In 1995 "I Am There" was featured on the television program "Angels II: Beyond the Light" on NBC. In talking about the poem, Jim said, "Of all the things I have ever written, 'I Am There' has meant the most to the most people. I wrote it in great anguish of spirit, out of a deep personal need. It has been reprinted many times, and people have written from all over the world to tell me how much it has meant to them."

Jim Freeman is Unity's poet laureate and has been described as a modern-day Transcendentalist, one whose philosophy carried on the tradition of David Thoreau,

"To the Unity School of Christianity with my gratitude for your prayers and my testimony that God was there."
—Jim Irwin, Apollo 15

Astronaut James B. Irwin visiting Jim Freeman at Unity Village.

introduction

Walt Whitman, and Ralph Waldo Emerson. His poems have touched the hearts of an estimated 500 million people, which if true certainly supports the notion that Jim Freeman has made a difference. He certainly has been published in some of the best magazines of his day, including *The New Yorker*. His books have been published by two of the most prestigious publishing houses, Harper & Row and Doubleday, as well as by Unity. His books have been translated into at least thirteen languages.

In one of the first books he ever wrote, *Happiness Can Be a Habit,* Jim wrote in the Foreword a piece called "Angels Sing in Me" that has become the title of this collection. "Angels sing in me" is the phrase that Jim used to describe his Muse, the creative power that moved through the universe and through him. One evening, after he had been writing, he got into bed with his wife and turned to her and said: "You know, honey, I'm a very lucky guy. Angels sing in me." And he knew in that moment, as he did each time Spirit moved through him, that he was "on to something." He got out of his bed and went back to his desk and wrote. What he wrote, you will read very shortly.

The angels that sang in Jim also will sing in you as you read this book. It is a rare privilege to get inside an author's head and heart and to feel the intense honesty and passionate longing of his soul that is there. That is what awaits you. So light a proverbial fire in your hearth and settle into your most comfortable chair and prepare to be entertained and comforted, challenged and changed forever. Angels like to do that to a person; I'm sure our poet would agree.

Angels within Unity are traditionally seen more as thought forms serving as messengers of God rather than as actual entities, but here we allow our poet his well-earned license. Besides, all poets see things metaphorically, through the eyes of their imagination; who is here to argue that that isn't a wiser way to look at the world?

I also want to acknowledge that the audiocassette *Angels Sing in Me: The Best of James Dillet Freeman*, which came out in 1996, has been a real source of inspiration for me. I've listened to it over and over again. To actually hear Jim Freeman reading his own poetry has been extremely helpful, and I am grateful to Susan Kavanaugh for her careful compilation and commentary throughout the cas-

12

sette. To some degree, you can even say that it is an abridged audiobook of this volume, and I urge readers to think of it that way.

I also want to thank Virginia Love, Jim's wife, for her generous loan of family photographs to use in this book. And I am grateful to Wendy Rumsey for her many encouragements and practical support, as I am to Angela Curran, Dan Rebant, Debbie Freeman, Pete Rhea, and Bill Dale as well as Rosemary Rhea, Laura Bennett, Robert Brumet, and Vickie Nelson for their many ways of helping me. Special thanks go to Kim West for identifying and supporting the need for this book. Also we must thank the many constituents who have written and called in to ask for a book to commemorate and honor this beloved man.

Last, I must thank James Dillet Freeman for leaving us a legacy of poems, essays, and stories that lives on even though our poet and author has left this stage of life. Even as he has exited, that very act has given his work, given his voice, fresh power and substance. Dare I say it, he has been given new visibility.

Michael A. Maday was editor of Unity House and is a member of the editorial board of *Unity Magazine*. An ordained Unity minister, he has served as anthologist and writer for *New Thought for a New Millennium*, to which James Dillet Freeman also contributed.

I.
Writing

"Poetry is the lightning of God ... prose produces light, but poetry strikes fire—and to live, we need fire! We need the fire of faith, the warmth of love. That is why metaphysics should be poetry. When it becomes poetry, it not only helps us to understand, it helps us to live, it helps us to be."

To Begin

I sat down to write,
and I asked myself,
"What shall I write?"
My heart said,
"Write about love."
But my mind said,
"Write about wisdom."
My heart did not argue with my mind,
it merely embraced my mind with love.
Then after a while
my mind spoke again and said,
"Love is wisdom."

Angels Sing in Me

Angels sing in me.

I rush to write down what I hear.

I carry a pad and pencil everywhere, for this singing may come at any hour in any place.

I must get it down quickly and turn it into words and phrases before it passes away, leaving no trace.

For the angels, I have noticed, hardly ever sing the same song twice—like God, they are original spirits and do not repeat themselves.

Usually the music comes in bursts and snatches—hardly a few notes together—a phrase, a line—that is all.

And I must turn this celestial strain I have caught, as the angels flew through my head, into a poem or a paragraph or even pages of writing.

This is hard.

The heavenly sounds get mixed with earthly ones—the angel song with my own.

All I can do is pray that my angels will return and look over my shoulder where I write and whisper a few more words in my ear.

So that the singing I heard you may hear too, for I pity all in this world who never hear an angel singing.

Poetry Is Song

When I was making a talk in Amarillo, Texas, a man showed me a letter. The woman who had written it had come to him a few days before. A doctor had just told her that her husband had an inoperable brain tumor and there was no hope. She would be left with two small children to support. The man who gave me the letter said: "I did not know what to say to her, but I happened to have a *Daily Word* on my desk. I gave her that." Now he had received this letter. In it she told how she was finding courage. What had helped her most, she said, was the poem on the back cover of *Daily Word*. She even quoted from it. The poem was one about a laughing mountain.

A woman I met in Birmingham, Alabama, told me a story about another poem, one I had written about imagining violets. "It had meant a lot to me when I first read it," she said, "so I kept it. One day I came home to discover that a neighbor had just lost her husband in an accident. They were dear friends and im-mediately I thought, Oh, I must go to her. But then I thought, What can I say? I could think of nothing else but your poem about violets. I took it out of the desk where I kept it and started across the yard to her house. This was in January. As I hurried along, I stumbled over something on the lawn. I looked down, and there was a small clump of violets in bloom! Violets don't bloom in Birming-ham in January any more than they do in Kansas City in March. But there they were. I went in and put that little clump of violets and your poem into her hand."

I am not sure how a laughing mountain or those imagined vio-lets said what needed to be said to help two women at a critical mo-ment of their lives.

Often people tell me what certain poems say to them. Some-times I get the poems out and read them to see if I can figure out how they meant that to those readers, but I hardly ever can.

But that is the very nature of poetry. What does a poem say? It says what it says to you!

When people ask me what a poem says, I can only tell them to read the poem. That is what I have to do.

The poem said to me what I wrote down. If I could have said it better, I would have written that.

A poem, however, is hardly ever obvious. A laughing mountain may say courage, and imagined violets may say peace and strength.

I may think I am writing about Christmas or bread or lilacs or bridges—and all the time I am really writing about life or about you or about me, only what I am saying cannot be effectively said in a more direct or abstract way.

This is why poetry is an ideal form of communication when one is trying to write about God. This is why the Bible and most of the great scriptures of the world are mainly poetic. The Hindus say that all one can say about God is, "He is." But a poem does not try to say what God is; instead it lets you feel what God is like.

What then should my poems do for you?

First of all, they should sing for you, and they should set you singing. Poetry is song. The whole universe moves in rhythm; our pulse dances, keeping time to the music of our central being. Let us give it tunes then to which it may dance in joy.

Also, I trust my poems will breathe courage. May a line here and there flash in your imagination like a spark and catch fire to your thoughts—to warm your heart for a passing moment, or perhaps to light a light in you that will cast a brightening ray down the long path of your life.

Above all, I hope my poems will help you to keep a sense of wonder, which is the ability to be perpetually surprised by the freshness of things. Without this, life runs down and turns into a daily dull repetition and humdrum succession of events.

Whether you read one poem or a hundred, I pray that you may always have a new sense of the wonder of God, a sense that you live in a world of wonders, and a sense that not the least of wonders is yourself.

The Way of the Heart

Everyone who writes hopes that what he writes will turn out to be a poem. He does not necessarily want to make words rhyme, but he wants his utterance to be one of truth and beauty and feeling, he wants it to be a beautiful and intense revelation of Truth—and this is what a poem is.

In their noblest moments, in their keenest insights, all of us are likely to become poets. It is not just happenstance that the King James Bible is the most beautiful English ever written or the Koran the most beautiful Arabic or the Bhagavad Gita the most beautiful Sanskrit. To express sublime thoughts, the heart cries out for sublime language.

Jesus was a poet. When they asked him what heaven is, he answered that it is like a mustard seed. That is a poet's answer. When he wanted to show God's relationship to us, he called God our Father. That is a poet's epithet. And there is no greater poem in literature than his Sermon on the Mount.

God might be thought of as a poet. For God was not content to expound abstract principles, but shaped them into the violets, clouds, stars, dew, redbirds, tigers, human beings, and all the rest of the infinite variety of fantastic, noble, original, unique things that form the world.

Many of us are so much a part of life that we take no time or thought to listen to what life has to say to us; we simply live. But some are listeners. They have time (or take time) to stand on a corner of the world and listen—to what the wind has to say in such a hurry, or the tree so patiently, or the cloud so briefly, or the flower in the wall, or the city street, or the people—oh, the lovely, beloved people!—or the "still small voice" within.

The poet is a listener. Everything is the speech of God, and the poet is God's interpreter. The poet listens and puts down what she hears. She listens without prejudice. She is as much concerned with what a mouse has to say as with what the President has to say or with what the Great Nebula in

Andromeda has to say. A mouse spoke to Bobbie Burns one day when he was plowing a field, and we are still reading—two hundred years later—what Burns wrote down.

Most of us are tied up in the logic of our own thinking; we have preconceived notions as to what things are and what can be expected from them. Not so the poet. She perfects her techniques, but she leaves her mind free, and she has a hospitable mind. She invites the Truth and expects the unexpected.

This is one of the great joys of writing poetry. I do not dictate to my mind what it should say. I leave it free, and I am often as much surprised at what I have to say as any reader is. A poem is as unpredictable as lightning.

Poetry is the lightning of God. Like the observer in the crow's nest of a ship, the poet has learned to see by lightning. And he speaks by lightning too, in lines and phrases rather than at length. If he writes a long work, it, too, comes by bursts and flashes; later he arranges these in orderly sequence. A single phrase of poetry may sometimes say more than many pages of prose, a single line as much as a book.

We think we live in an age of prose. But I have noticed that in a time of need, it is likely to be some line of poetry that rises to our mind—perhaps a line we learned by heart in school and thought we had forgotten years before. It is by heart that we have to learn poetry, for poetry is the way of the heart.

Poetry is as intense as life. The wind is not flat, the sea dull, love colorless, God an abstraction—we experience life keenly, with all our faculties. And poetry, like life, is vivid, colorful, concrete. It makes the truth stand out in sharp relief.

Poetry has more dimensions than prose. God is not just a truth you can think about; God is a faith you can feel, a presence you can experience. Poetry enables you to feel and experience God as well as think about Him. The poet does not so much want you to say, "Now I see what God is"; she wants you to say, "Now I see God!"

Prose produces light, but poetry strikes fire—and to live, we need fire! We need the fire of faith, the warmth of love. That is why metaphysics should be poetry. When it becomes poetry, it not only helps us to understand, it helps us to live, it helps us to be.

That is why whenever I sit down to write I pray that what I write may turn out to be a poem—

that is, an intense and beautiful revelation of Truth. I believe God is. I believe that God's spirit is in us. I believe that faith and love and prayer are life. Because I hold these truths passionately, I want to express them eloquently, for I want you, too, to hold them passionately. I want you to know them not only in your mind but with every fiber of your being. I want you to *be* these truths. I believe that they are life to you.

That is why whenever I sit down to write, I pray that what I write may turn out to be a poem—that is, an **intense** and **beautiful** revelation of Truth.

II.
Purpose

O God ... I have only to seek, and I come on Your truths.
I have only to cry out, and Your love embraces me.
I have only to be what I am meant to be, and I am one with what You are.

I'm a Seeker

I'm a seeker, an asker, a knocker at the door. I've never been able to believe something just because some authority pronounces it as true. I have to find out for myself, or at least try to find out. All my life I've gone to God and asked God many questions, and most of the time God's answered me with many questions of His own, as He answered Job.

Lord, Help Me to Help People Not to Hurt So Much

Ever since I was a little boy, I have sensed how much pain there is in the world. I remember one night riding home in a streetcar, and there was no one else in the car except a black child about my size. There was a motorman, of course, but he was just part of the streetcar, which says a great deal about how we often think of one another. As I rode in the brightly lighted streetcar through the dark city so crowded with so many people, each one trudging down his own special street I hardly knew the name of and probably would never walk along, each one dwelling behind his own curtained windows of rooms I would never see, each one a stranger to all but a handful, each one going his own personal way, caught in his own web of habit and happenstance—all so unknown to me but all so like me, suddenly a sense of identity with all other human beings poured overwhelmingly over me. I stared at the other boy, so like me, yet so unlike me, and suddenly I was the little black child in the big white world. Perhaps it was only my own pain and my own feelings of rage and rejection that I found myself projecting as his, but I found myself praying, "Lord, help me to help people not to hurt so much!" I have prayed that prayer all my life: "O God, help me to help people not to hurt so much. Help me to help people to live."

The Fruit of God

I would I might become the human tree
of God and give with no thought to withhold
from life whatever gifts I have in me;
the fruit of God is better than fine gold.
I plant my thought-trees in the field of mind,
trees of imagination, trees of reason,
but would not have them bear after their kind;
I would have them bear God's fruit in His own season.
For sometimes there appears upon the bough
a harvest no man had foreknowledge of,
a fruit no tongue has tasted until now,
the golden apples of God's perfect love.
I would not give out of what I possess
but out of God's exuberance and excess.

A Minister

What does it mean to be a minister?

It means to make yourself small so that others may feel large.

It means to make yourself a servant so that others may feel their mastery.

It means to give so that those who lack may receive.

It means to love so that those who feel unloved may have someone who never rejects them, someone with whom they can always identify.

It means to hold out your help to those who ask and deserve help—and also to those who do not ask or deserve it. It means always to be there when you are needed, yet never to press yourself on another when you are not wanted.

It means to stay at peace so that those who are contentious will have someone to whom they can turn to stabilize themselves.

It means to keep a cheerful outlook so that those who are easily cast down may have someone to lift them up.

It means to keep faith and to keep on keeping faith even when you yourself find little reason for believing, so that those who have no faith can find the courage to live.

It means not merely to live a life of prayer, but to turn your prayers into life—more life for you, more life for those to whom you minister.

It means to be God-centered and human-hearted, to involve yourself in humanity, and to keep your vision on divinity—and so draw forth in all around you the human form divine.

It means to share in the great moments of life—in birth and sickness and marriage and death—and at all these times, whether of crisis or of celebration, to bring comfort and a blessing and, above all, a sense of a Presence that sometimes we cannot see and of a Meaning that often we overlook.

That is what it means to be a minister of God and a minister to humanity.

Footprints

Footprints—
in the new snow
I follow them.

God, too, makes footprints—
across nothingness.

Sunrise and sunset,
day and night,
the Earth and Sun and stars,
flowers of spring,
summer harvests,
autumn leaves,
winter snow—
these are God's footprints.

Order and beauty and growth,
healing for the body,
new thoughts for the mind,
peace for the spirit—
I see where God has been.

And in me,
I trace God's footprints
by my aspirations.

Lord, Lord,
make my life
Your footprint.

Life's Child

When I was a school boy, I confess
my favorite subject was recess,
and still I do not find it hard
to loiter in my heart's schoolyard
entranced by all the things that are
such bright adornments of this star.
I pray I shall not ever be
so grown up that the child in me
will have no wish to run and play
and sing and dance the hours away.
Oh, may I sometimes in my mind
leap up and leave my cares behind
and live as if I truly were
life's child and chief inheritor.

III.

meaning

Perfection's Imminence

I have gone down a road and had a sense
suddenly of perfection's imminence.
The same leaves trembled in the sunlight, still
it was as if I had come round a hill
and looked for the first time at reality.
Men live on the edge of a world they never see,
but sometimes I have drawn aside the screen
and felt through to the real and serene
beyond the world of forms whose shadows pass
across my mind as in a looking glass.
Then I have been as in another land;
I have stood upon the verge of beauty and
felt a reality too beautiful to bear
about to reveal itself through the electric air.

A World Alive

Life has meaning. It has meaning in an absolute and ultimate sense.

This does not mean that it has meaning in a fixed and rigid sense.

Need ultimates be fixed and absolutes unchanging?

If the only meanings you can accept are ultimate and everlasting, I believe you are in for ultimate and everlasting disappointment. I hope so. I would hate to be in a world where I knew everything there is to know about it. As I look around me this spring morning, when the fields are green with grass and golden with dandelions and the air is white with windblown petals and passing clouds, I feel certain this is no such world.

In this world every answer always leads to two new questions. And of all human capacities, none is more to be desired than the capacity for wonder.

I pray that you are exercising yours. I pray that I may never lose mine. May I never pridefully believe I *know* more than I *do not know*—about anything.

I know so little even about that which is closest to me—myself. If I know so little about me, I must know even less about you. And still less about other living forms and about the atoms and galaxies I have never seen but the scientists tell me are there.

I am convinced that the universe we live in is alive, not dead. The more I write, the more I have come to feel that perhaps this is the main reason I write. To say what I feel needs to be said over and over again. To say it especially in this time when we have gotten to thinking of the world in fixed, mechanical terms.

We live in a living world.

Dear reader, do you hear what I am saying?

Your world is not dead.

Your world is not a box with fixed and rigid dimensions.

Your world is not constructed like a machine and operated on mechanical principles.

Your world is alive.

And since it is alive, it is growing.

And since it is growing, all the

measurements you may make of it and all the observations you may observe about it and all the limitations you may place on it—and on yourself!—will pass away.

Be!

We live in an age when many feel that life is meaningless. Skeptics look at things and see no reason for believing; for every reason they have a counterreason.

But life answers the skeptic where reason may not. For life says to him: *Live! Be!*

We do not need speculation to prove that life has meaning any more than we need a discourse on the laws of light to prove that a rainbow or a sunset has meaning.

Asking the reason for life is like asking the reason for a crocus or love. Life needs no reason for being. It is its own reason for being.

The meaning of music is not to be found in a music book. To find the meaning of music, we have to listen to music—and even then, we may not be able to put its meaning into words. Music has a meaning that words are often inadequate to express.

Life is like music. Its Composer had a thought for which words were inadequate. So God said, simply, "Let there be!" All the music of life is the expression of God's thought.

We may not have found God, but that does not mean that God is not there. We may not be able to work problems in calculus, but they can be worked. We do not have to know the answer to know that there is an answer.

Outside my window a redbird fills the morning with its singing. It does not sing because it knows the answer. Its song is the answer. Above me a squirrel flings itself from bough to bough. It does not leap because it knows the answer. Its leap is the answer. The rosebush in my garden unfolds a perfect rose. It does not produce the rose because it knows the answer. Its rose is the answer.

Life cries to me with ten thousand tongues that it is meaningful. Morning cries it with sunlight and birdsongs and pink rosebud clouds. Noon cries it from a brazen mouth of fire, evening with the still small voice of quietness, night with darkness and the lights of all the stars. Spring shouts it like a hallelujah chorus. The horns of summer blow it across the groves and meadows.

Fall's gold and scarlet fifes repeat it on the burning hills. It rumbles on the drums of winter under the brooding snows. Storms cry out its meaning no less than tranquil seasons do.

Every blade of grass crackles it out like an old radio, pushing up under my feet. Every seed affirms it, the sound of the cracking of shells and the splitting of husks, the thud of fruit dropping on the earth, the silence of the tree bare to the winter wind. Mole underground, eagle in the air, striped tiger, horned rhinoceros, squeaking mouse, cawing magpie—all the infinite menagerie of God inform me that life has meaning, a meaning vast and wonderful, as beautiful and strange as the world of form itself.

Oh, the crack-crowding, heart-warming, death-destroying wonder of life! The swarming, sprouting, growing, proliferating wonder! It drifts to and fro in the air. Every inch of earth is packed with it. Let the merest rain fall, and the desert blooms. Even in the dark of the ocean, it abounds.

I sense that there is nothing that is not unique, special, important, meaningful. The smallest particle is power incarnate. There is no atom, no merest speck of life that is not pregnant with all the possibilities of the universe. There is so much meaning in the least living thing that its obliteration (if this were possible, which it is not) would

The meaning of music

is not to be found in a music book. To find the meaning of music, we have to listen to music—and even then, we may not be able to put its meaning into words. Music has a meaning that words are often inadequate to express.

Life is like music.

make such a void in the heart of God that infinity would be swallowed up in it.

Yet all this world of forms, wrought with such cunning that no two atoms in it are the same, is only the shadow of the wonder and beauty that are there. Strip away the wonder of form and a yet greater wonder appears. For the world of forms that stretches out around us, shifting, fair, new, strange, familiar, passing, passionate, is not dense and corporeal but in reality a world of light. At the heart of all that is, there is fire. We live in a world of light. We are ourselves light. If the many seem wonderful, how much more wonderful is the One! Are you the least? You are no less than the greatest. Even "the least of these" is God.

I have only to look, I have only to reach, I have only to taste, I have only to feel, I have only to live—to know that the world is a work more wonderful than anything I can imagine it to be, anything I do imagine it to be! The wildest wonderment of all poets, dreamers, inventors, speculators that have ever lived is as nothing compared to the wonderment that is the world. The world is God's wonderment, infinite intelligence compounding its infinity, the joy of eternity delighting in itself.

And when I consider humanity, our dreams and deeds, the deeps in us, the heights in us—frail as flesh, fragile as mind and spirit, yet challenging darkness, even death; not sure of our way but venturing forward, not unafraid but not turning back, not free from pain but with faith that we can master it, not beyond selfishness yet struggling to subdue ourselves; falling yet keeping the vision, loving life yet able to love truth more than life—then it is as if I stand upon a storm-swept plain at night, and suddenly, the clouds split, and behold, the lightning of God! For when I consider humanity, I catch a glimpse of God in whose image we are made.

Listen to life, and you shall hear the voice of life crying: *Be!*

What shall you be?

Be what you were made to be!

You were made to be alive. You were made to be joy. You were made to be a child of God. God made you in His image. The impress of Spirit is on your every living cell.

For this alone, all things were made—to be! Life is not to be explained in terms of aims and ends and goals, but only in terms of living. Life has goals and a goal,

I have only to look, I have only to reach, I have only to taste, I have only to feel, I have only to live—to know that **the world is a work more wonderful than anything I can imagine it to be**, anything I do imagine it to be! The wildest wonderment of all poets, dreamers, inventors, speculators that have ever lived is as nothing compared to the wonderment that is the world.

but its meaning and worth do not depend on this fact. How shall we explain life in terms of ends? There is no end that is not a starting point.

Is it wonderful to be a grown man or woman? It is also wonderful to be a child. The joy of arrival is great, but so is the joy of the journey.

Life is made up of wonderful differences and different wonders; all of life is wonderful. Let us not say of one that it is more or less than another, but let us find meaning and worth in all. Today is the actualization of all yesterdays, the potentiality of all tomorrows.

Today needs no reason for being. It is its own reason for being. Sufficient that it is today.

Life needs no reason for being. It is its own reason for being. Sufficient that it is life.

meaning

You need no reason for being. You are your own reason for being. Sufficient that you are you.

God loves you for what you are, not for what you have done or have not done. What are you? You are God's child. That is your reason for being.

You are born a king. What ambition can a king have to become something more than what he already is? He can only aspire to be the best possible king.

It is as if the rose should cry out, "For what was I born?" O rose, you were born to be a perfect rose! O human, you were born to be a perfect expression of God!

Aim at the highest, though you may not hit it. If you never aim beyond your reach, you will not grow. To be is to grow, and to grow is to aim beyond your reach. Growth is aspiration, and aspiration is the impulse to be what you were born to be.

Life is made for the high aimers. They are the true aimers. It is they who make all growth possible.

O human, you are the spiritual seed of God! Grow as a tree grows, rising out of yourself as a tree rises out of itself.

A redwood seed is very small to grow into such a gigantic tree. You are more than a redwood tree. For it has height and breadth and depth, but you have other dimensions. You are mind. You are spirit.

O human, you were made to be the perfect expression of God!

God said, *"Be!"*

How Can I Know?

How can I know God is? How can I know the world makes sense? How can I know there is a purpose in living? How can I know?

These are the questions of all of us. When we seek for an answer to them, where shall we look?

Look out at the vastness of things. See the stars blossoming like the unfolding petals of a rose and you sense the moving order that rules the depths of space. Look at the least blade of grass—out of sunlight and water and air, it makes new life!—and you sense the inconceivable intelligence that works in the least of things.

And more than intelligence! If we could get at the heart of things, a heart is what we would find—something much more like heart than mind, much more like love than law, much more like beauty than reason.

Take rainbows, for example. The Bible says a rainbow is a token of God's covenant with humankind. There is a reason for rain, but not for a rainbow. The universe would operate as effi-ciently without one, only not so beautifully, that is all. Only the Spirit of divine delight could have conceived rainbows, the same Spirit that made butterflies—those flowers with wings! And indeed all the infinite, outpouring, heaped-up, overflowing variety of things bursting the seams of the world makes me know absolutely that something is at work here so alive that life is too weak a word to de-scribe it. The Spirit of God is not just life, not just intelligence. It is sheer exuberance, the love of joy in living! It never makes two blades of grass alike. It crowds ev-ery crack with growing things and space with universes.

Clouds form and dissolve, birds sing, insects rise, leaves tremble, flowers unfold—all is change, ac-tivity, livingness. You may be part of this livingness. The universe is as a web, beautifully woven; its threads spiraling out, linking ev-ery living thing, even every atom, so intimately so perfectly that no least thread, no least point at the perimeter, can be touched, but the whole web vibrates in harmony.

The Spirit of God is not just life, not just intelligence. It is sheer exuberance, the love of joy in living! **It never makes two blades of grass alike.** It crowds every crack with growing things and space with universes.

You can be one with this oneness of things. You need not be little and alone, isolated and meaningless. You are part of life.

One with life, you lose your sense of separateness, your sense of self. No bird flies, but your thought takes flight; no bird sings, but a song is in your heart. You are brother to the fly and cousin to the cricket. You are as much a part of life as a cloud is part of the air. Who shall say where cloud ends and air begins? At its edges, it is some of both. At your edges, you are part of all that is, part of the livingness of life.

In the infinite flux of life, there is no separateness, there is only whole-ness—only the many faces of the One. Give yourself to living, and you will find meaning, for you will be one with the One life.

Where shall you look to see God?

Look at yourself. Do you see a mortal, flesh-and-blood creature? That is not what I see when I look at you. I see a spiritual being. Why do I think you are spiritual? For one thing, because you have to live as if you were.

If we know what makes a creature happy, we know its true nature. To be happy, a swallow must fly. So we say it is a bird of flight. To be happy, a thrush must sing. So we say it is a songbird. To be happy, a person must try to satisfy spiritual desires. What else then can we say, save that a person is Spirit!

If man were a mortal, flesh-and-blood creature with only physical needs to satisfy, then a life spent in satisfying these needs should be the most sat-isfactory of lives. But it is the least satisfactory. Something in you is more than flesh-and-blood. Something in you is wings. Something in you is song. Something in you is Spirit.

What are the longings of your heart, the aspirations of your mind? Consider them well, for they reveal the pattern in which you were formed. They are the voice of your true Self, demanding expression. For this, you were formed before Abraham was! And all the forces of Heaven and Earth combine to bring this true pattern in you to fruition.

There is something in you that tells you you were meant for more than all you have achieved, no matter what that may be; something in you that will be satisfied with nothing less than greatness. It may settle for less, but it is not satisfied. It may be covered over with years of dusty mediocrity, of compromise and resignation to necessity. But it is there.

Something in you is Spirit, and it hungers and thirsts after spiritual things—righteousness, usefulness, selflessness. It is not content merely to live; it has to live well!

You are more than body, more than mind. These may be altered, but there is something in you that cannot be altered. It is immortal. It is incorruptible. How do I know that this is there? Because I have caught glimpses of it. I have looked with love's eyes. It is not only when I look at Jesus that I see God. I see God when I look at every person.

Sometimes we think we would believe if only we had a sign. "Give me a revelation, God!" we cry. "O Lord, let pass a miracle!"

This I believe: anyone who sincerely asks for signs will have signs. Pray, pray steadfastly, and you will have prayers answered.

But do not seek for God to show Himself in supernatural ways and forget that He is constantly showing Himself in natural ways. God is the unusual, no doubt; but God is the usual too. Do not seek the burning bush and miss the bushes glowing with bloom in your own backyard. Do not look for God in the heavens and pass God by in your neighbor without speaking.

Do you seek a miracle? What is more a miracle than morning, when the light comes streaming back to Earth? Or spring, when death is overcome by every greening clod? A star is a miracle, and you live on one. Thought is a miracle, and it is closest to you of all that is. You are a miracle. Every moment of your life is more packed with miracles than the Bible.

It is all right to ask for signs, but to build on signs is to build on

43

sands, for it is to build on appearances. We have to go deeper than appearances, even good appearances; else the first adversity will sweep our faith away. We cannot build much of a faith on the fact that we happen to be having a comfortable, pain-free existence.

But there is a knowledge of God, there is a faith in life, that has nothing to do with appearances. For, fundamentally, God and life are not something we know with our brain but in our bones, in the very marrow of our bones, the marrow of our spirit. I do not need to convince the hare that bursts from under my feet and bounds quickly away that life is good. He knows. He may be wet and cold and alone and shelterless and hungry; yet he knows. Every frantic leap he makes is a living affirmation of life.

The hare knows—and deep down so do we all—that one moment of life is worth infinitely more than all the nonlife (if such there could be) in the world. If eternity had no other meaning, it came alive with meaning the moment life appeared in it.

For myself, I have never known with such absolute certainty that God is and life is meaningful and purposive as I knew at a time when appearances were declaring the exact opposite. My brain was full of doubts, but I knew with more than brain. God was there, that is all. Underneath were the everlasting arms. I felt

Do you seek a miracle? What is more a miracle than morning, when the light comes streaming back to Earth? Or spring, when death is overcome by every greening clod? A star is a miracle, and you live on one. Thought is a miracle, and it is closest to you of all that is. You are a miracle. Every moment of your life is more packed with miracles than the Bible.

the arms. I recognized the presence of God was there; that is the only way I can describe what I experienced. At the moment I was deepest down, I was also highest up. I knew God not by believing in Him or reasoning through to Him. I simply knew God.

If you want to know the stars, do you study astronomy books? Do you think about stars? Perhaps, but most of all you go out and commune with them—warm and glowing in the dark. And on a dark night when no star appears, the stars may be more meaningful and real than ever. If you live close enough to the stars, they go right on shining in you.

So it is with God. God is not something you have sometimes, if you work hard to find Him. God is in you, and you are in God.

When you give yourself to life, you have not reasons for living, but life itself. When you give yourself to God, you have not thoughts about God, but God Himself.

How can you know God is? How can you know the world makes sense? How can you know there is a purpose in living? How can you know?

You can know God as you know the stars are shining on a cloudy night, as you know someone you love is in the next room.

Give yourself to life in love and with faith. For then you live not on the surface but at the heart of things. And the heart of things is the heart of God.

45

We Have to Live Here and Now

We have to find our meaning living this usual life. If we keep seeking it somewhere else, it will always elude us. One of the great Zen masters is asked, "What is *satori*?" (another word for *nirvana*). He answers, "Walk on." If we try to put this in our own Western terms, we might say something like: We have to live here and now. Earth is also heaven.

Many years ago I wrote a little piece of verse as I walked across the fields of Unity Village. When I wrote it, I had no thought about samsara or nirvana. I'm not sure I'd ever heard of either of them. I was just walking on, thinking what I was thinking, feeling what I was feeling, being what I was being. But today, as I was thinking about this Eastern truth, *samsara* is *nirvana*, I suddenly realized that my little poem expresses it beautifully. That's the great luck of being a poet. You walk about listening for the truth and sometimes you hit the mark without taking aim. This is the verse. It is called, "Had We the Eyes":

How fair a world around us lies,
heaven unfurled, had we the eyes
to see the worth of all that is;
like heaven Earth is also His.
How can the rose, more than the clod
from which it grows, embody God.

Isn't this what Jesus is telling us when he says, "The kingdom of heaven is within you" or as other versions of the Bible put it, "The kingdom of heaven is in the midst of you"? The kingdom of heaven is among the heaven-hearted, wherever they are, and that is the only place it will ever be.

We're here to build the new Jerusalem. Not somewhere else. Not later. Not in some different mode of manifestation. Not on some different level of existence. We're here to bring forth God's perfection now. I believe this. I believe I am here to transform the world into a better place to live. You can't work all your life as I have, in a great prayer ministry like Silent Unity where your whole reason for being is to help people who need help, without believing this and doing all you can to bring it about. My great prayer has been, "Lord, help me to help people to be what they are meant to be."

Upon This Flame

I watched the rocket flight.
I saw men ride
a thundering plume of flame
serenely out of sight.
They rose astride
a million fiery horses yoked in one dancing blaze
till they flew free
of all our slow earth-crawl and weighty ways.
Like a wind, the ship's wash came
shaking the earth and me.

And then I saw

the first man rubbing firesticks till his straw
glowed and puffed smoke.
I watched how he leaned and blew
till the fire broke
and the flame crept, leapt, soared, roared
not only in the straw but in his eyes.

And then I knew

that the fire by which men rise
and leave old worlds behind
leaps not so much in the pale
straw or the rocket's tail
as in the mind.

Upon this flame man flies.

IV.

God

What God Is Like

I did not know what God is like
until a friendly word
came to me in an hour of need—
and it was God I heard.

I did not know what God is like
until I heard love's feet
on errands of God's mercy
go up and down life's street.

I did not know what God is like
until I felt a hand
clasp mine and lift me when alone
I had no strength to stand.

I think I know what God is like,
for I have seen the face
of God's son looking at me
from all the human race.

Because He Is Love

Who of us does not have times when he thinks he is not good enough to go to God for help? But God does not help me because He approves or disapproves of what I am doing.

God helps me because He is God. Because He is life. Because He is love.

God does not help me because I am good.

God helps me because He is good.

God does not help me because I deserve help or love me because I deserve love.

Do you love only those who have no flaws? And would you think that you can love where God cannot? Love sees things perfect in spite of flaws.

I do not have to be perfect to lay hold of love's perfection.

God does not answer my prayers to reward me because I have been good or deny my prayers to punish me because I have been bad.

God does not strike a bargain.

God does not work for pay.

God gives.

God does not wait until I give myself to Him to give Himself to me. He seeks me even when I flee from Him. And whither may I flee from Him who is everywhere at hand?

God has me in His heart, whether I have Him in my heart or not.

I do not have to be the most willing for Him to choose me or the most capable for Him to use me.

It is not only good people God has used to do His good.

It is not only brave people God has used to win His victories.

It is not only righteous people God has used to establish right.

So I hold out my heart and I pray, "God, whatever my heart may have felt, love through it."

I hold out my mind and I pray, "God, whatever my mind may have thought, think through it."

I hold out my hands and I pray, "God, whatever my hands may have done, act through them."

For I know that God does not give His strength only to the strong or His wisdom only to the wise or His joy only to the joyful or His blessing only to the blest.

God does not help me because of what I am.

God helps me because of what He is.

God is love.

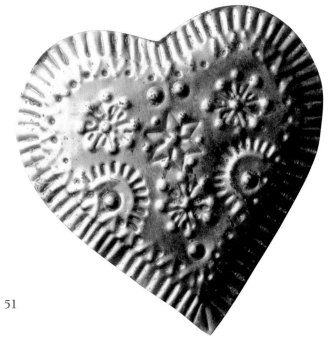

Presence

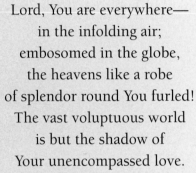

Lord, You are everywhere—
in the infolding air;
embosomed in the globe,
the heavens like a robe
of splendor round You furled!
The vast voluptuous world
is but the shadow of
Your unencompassed love.

You are in everything—
brute, bird, and blossoming.
You lap my limbs with grace;
your likeness fills my face;
I seek you and I find
You hidden in my mind:
You in my inmost part,
I inmost in Your heart!

Love's Purple Patches

I think that God is love because
He makes things lovelier than laws
call for. God slips into the batches
of life's gray paint, love's purple patches:
sunsets, bluebirds, butterflies,
rainbows in rain—God likes surprise.
Take lilacs—just the leaves would be
a heart-shaped miracle to see,
but God adds flowers in spring, a foam
of purple bees on a honeycomb,
a violet swarm of stars that cling
in galaxies of glittering,
and lilacs are not leaf and bloom,
but utter attar, sheer perfume,
fragrance! Lilacs tell me love
is what things are constructed of.
I note how God has wrapped this globe
in lilac air like a seamless robe.
And I sense, no less than lilacs, you
and I, at heart, are love's stuff too.

Of Gnats' Wings

Life is a many-colored wonder, the flowering of a creative spirit so original, spontaneous, exuberant, and free that it has never repeated itself since worlds began.

It has not made two stars alike. It has not made two human beings alike. It has not made two cells alike. It has not made two atoms—no, not two electrons!—alike.

If we could magnify the most minute particles until they looked as large as you and I, we would see they are as different as you and I.

This is one of the reasons I believe in God. If the world were the work of mechanical forces, mechanical forces would long ago have worked out ways for mechanically mass-producing everything. We would live in an assembly-line world where stars and hearts would be stamped out, each one exactly like every other.

But we don't. We live in a handmade world. Each star and each heart is the work of something that insists on making an original production of everything it makes, no matter how small or how momentary.

Nothing is unimportant to it, so it has designed a world in which everything can be itself.

One thing certain about whatever it is that made the world, it is clearly a creative spirit delighting in its own creativity. Whatever it is that made the world, it is much more like mind than like machinery.

But what a Mind—so infinite in its capacity that it can give as much thought to an atom as to a star and make a gnat's wings as uniquely beautiful as the wings of the mightiest of its angels!

God is not the ultimate engineer but the original artist.

And God's work is never a still life but always life alive, the moving formlessness that ever seeks to find itself in form and the living form that ever seeks to lose itself in formlessness.

"Whom My Soul Loveth"

"I will rise now, and go about the city; In the streets and in the broadways I will seek him whom my soul loveth."

I have sought God in the streets of the world, in people, and in my own soul. Have I seen God?

I have seen snow falling, the spring green pushing upward, the summer flowers standing tall, the grain yellow lingering on in the autumn fields, the fruit burdening the orchards. I have felt the glory of the Sun. I have heard the feet of the rain running among the leaves. I have listened to the conversation of ancient trees. Night after night I have watched the steadfast stars and ever-changing Moon. The red-bird has wakened me, and I have fallen asleep to the crickets' tune. The majesty of mountains, the wonder of the sea, the stretch of valleys, the flight of the sky—all these I have seen.

Are these God? No, but they are the garments of God.

I have felt the wonder of life; its patient experimenting; its outward, upward striving; its eternal unfoldment. I have heard the laughter of children. I have seen the look in a mother's eyes. I have watched lovers strolling hand in hand and heart in heart. I have known men brave enough to die for one another and selfless enough to live for one another. I have felt what a wonderful thing it is to be a human being.

Is this God? No, but it is the personality of God.

I have been alone under the sky when suddenly I was one with all the beauty and wonder and glory of the world. The sky was not high enough; the horizons were not wide enough to hold my heart. I reached out through all the galaxies and nebulae, the infinite stretches of space, and I knew that they were in me and of me.

I have walked down a street crowded with strangers when suddenly they were not strangers and I felt myself expand and take them in. I felt their loneliest longings, their loftiest aspirations, their hopes and fears, their love and faith and joy. I was the self that transcends self, the larger Self that is not bound by space and time, the Self that knows that it is one

55

God

with the reality in all people.

I have gone into a quiet room, shut the doors of the senses, turned within, and found the peace that passes understanding, the stillness that is the very heart of stillness, the place where there is nothing at all; yet I am one with all that is.

Is this God? No, but it is the presence of God.

Where is God?

Search for God through the crowded city streets. Seek God in the peaceful countryside. Penetrate into the nucleus of the atom. Follow the curve of emptiness. Go to the end of time. God will be there. Wherever you are, God is.

Know, you who seek God, that He seeks you more steadfastly. God seeks you. God loves you. God will not leave you alone. You could not walk alone, not for a moment, not in the darkest night. Though you stretched not out your hand, yet your hand would be in God's. Though you held not out your heart, yet God's heart would infold you.

"I am sought of *them* that asked not for me; I am found of *them* that sought me not."

What is God? Can the eternal be less than infinite? God is the infinite livingness of life that is in all and through all and under all, ever seeking to express itself.

Some seek to catch God in a net of words, but God is more than a word. God is more than any thought that a man's mind can hold, yet God is the least thought that springs there. God is the first cry uttered by a newborn child, yet God is more than all the utterances of all the theologians.

God is more than all thought, all feeling, and all vision. God is the life that reveals that there is no death. God is the love that transforms hate into constructive energy. God is the intelligence that lifts ignorance into an understanding of Himself, of human beings, and of the universe.

O child of God, God is the truth of your own being!

Size

How vast a universe! On every side
crowded with worlds like ours it rushes out
into a darkness infinitely wide.
Who, looking at the vastness, does not doubt
man's meaning sometimes, seeing him so small
beside the flaming swarms of stars and suns?
How can the Lord, having to care for all
this glory, find time for such little ones?
But when I feel dwarfed by the vastness of
the world, I think how God, whose throne is space
and footstool is the stars, is also love
and of my heart has made His dwelling place.
How little God must have regard for size
who looks upon us with a Father's eyes!

V.

Life

A Beauty on the Land

There lies a beauty on the land,
but it is hard to understand
what is the glory in the sky
and on the stranger passing by.
The small sun does not rise or set;
the pavement glistens onyx-wet;
the little lights shine here and there;
a winter damp is in the air.
Yet all the gray familiar places,
all the streets and all the faces,
wear a look of faraway.
It is an ordinary day,
yet everywhere I look I find
a beauty that I passed by blind
an hour ago. Sometimes I think
we spend our life on beauty's brink
and never open up our eyes
to see how warm, how close it lies.

I Am God's Song

Perhaps I am most like a song.

What is a song?

A song is a thought in the imagination of its composer, an unheard music of the mind.

A song is words and notes set down on a sheet of music paper.

A song is a sweet undulation of sounds for a little time in a certain place.

And a song is also the singer singing, a mind and body expressing themselves.

I am the song and the sound and the singer.

You will hear me again and again in different keys, in different voices, whistled and chanted and hummed, sometimes only a few bars, sometimes sung over and over. The singer may sing imperfectly, yet I am always the same perfect song, imagined music in the mind of my Composer, written down in the Eternal's music book, flawless and complete.

I am God's song.

Listen for me.

You are God's song.

Listen.

The World Is Not What the World Seems

The world is not what the world seems. Surely you realize that. You and I are living in the midst of a mystery, and it's great. It's not a mystery because it doesn't have meaning; it's a mystery because it has so much meaning we can't grasp it. We haven't come up yet to the place where we can do that; we've only come up to here.

> Life has set me down in the midst of a mystery.
>
> It seems beyond my fathoming …
>
> Yet this much I see clearly—the mystery is not mystery because it is meaningless but because it is meaningful. It is not because things have so little meaning, but because they mean so much that I cannot grasp the meaning.
>
> How shall an inchworm comprehend a continent?
>
> But let the inchworm measure the mystery of a leaf or two, and it may turn into a butterfly and master even the mystery of air.
>
> And if an inchworm can turn into a butterfly, who shall say what a butterfly may become?
>
> I am God's inchworm and God's butterfly.
>
> O God, I inch my mind across the mystery that is my world, measuring it as best I may. Sometimes, if only for a moment, I encounter a meaning that is like light and an assurance that is like love.
>
> Then, though I cannot see the meaning clearly, I know that whatever the meaning is, it is not less but more. And whatever I am, I am more too.

What Is a Tree?

Life is much like a tree. We speak of the tree of life, and it is no mean symbol.

What is a tree?

If I asked you, I imagine you would talk to me about spreading branches and green leaves; you might tell me about its roots and trunk or speak to me of shade and fruit. If you are a botanist, you would speak to me in many-syllabled, scientific terms.

But what if I asked a bird that flies above it and perches in its branches to sing or sleep?

I wonder if you could find a tree from a bird's description of it. I wonder if you could even find a forest of trees.

What if I asked the ant I see scurrying up its trunk and running from twig to twig as it herds the aphids that feed on the leaves? What is a tree to an ant? I wonder if an ant may not see a tree as we see a landscape. Is every leaf a tree?

Or suppose I asked the vine that has grown up into the branches, wound its tendrils around the outstretched twigs, and is vying with the tree for light and life?

Or the worm deep down in the dark earth that has spent all its life gnawing on a root?

Or suppose I asked the tree itself!

The tree is the tree, the same tree to all of us—or is it the same?

Man and bird and ant and vine and squirrel and worm and tree—we do not know how to exchange ideas. But if we could communicate, I believe we would be like the blind men and the elephant. Each of us would have experienced the tree in such a different way that none of us would imagine we were speaking of the same object.

There is a real tree, and it is—shade to the man, home to the bird, a fertile forest to the ant, support to the vine, food to the worm, and tree to the tree.

The real tree is—wave particles? I like that. Consciousness? I like that too. These are the very up-to-date ways of describing reality. We'll find other ways tomorrow, for we had other ways yesterday.

For everything we say about anything—even one of the least—is not enough.

The Infinite One is expressing Himself in a tree. Say whatever you may say a tree is; there remains an infinity still to be said.

The tree is.

But what it is depends as much on what you are as on what the tree may happen to be.

So it is with the tree of life.

A Jigsaw Puzzle

Life is much like a jigsaw puzzle. Many of us look at the huge heap of jumbled pieces piled helter skelter on the table. Some pieces upside down, some turned around, most of them hidden in the pile, so we do not even see all the pieces; we see only a few on the surface.

Some of us scarcely examine the puzzle; we just stumble through the higgledy-piggledy disorder of day-to-day existence.

Some find a few sections put together by somebody else, perhaps somebody long ago, and we are satisfied with what was found. "I have faith that this is what the puzzle means," we intone.

Some, noting that pieces of the outside rim have to have one straight edge, look for these pieces and work with these because they are easiest to work with. When we have fitted a few together, we feel satisfied that we have found the meaning, even though it is a rim kind of meaning that has only one side.

Others of us spend our life piecing pieces and meaning together—laboriously sometimes, sometimes by good fortune or sudden insight.

And we catch a glimpse of—dare we say what? Yes, as long as we know that whatever we say, as we work on with the puzzle, we will have more to say. If what we have found seems to be flowers, we will find as we work on that what looked like flowers was really the plumage of birds. But further along, we will see that what we took to be birds is more likely clouds glowing in the sun. But later yet, we may see that what seemed to be clouds is in reality angels. And after angels?

The creative spirit of life has not given us a cheap puzzle to pass an easy hour. This life is many-dimensioned and ever-changing. Whatever we make it out to be, it will be yet more.

Life Is Change

If there's one great truth about life, it is that life is change.
As we live, we all move from level to level in consciousness. We go up a path, and as we go, things change and we change. It is as when we move from city to city; we can never go back. We may think we can go back. We may wish to go back. We may look back with longing and think to ourselves, Ah, that was the good life then! We may even go back to what we thought was the city we left. But it will never be there, not the city we remember.

Once you come up a step, you can never go back. When you start to go back, you quickly find that you can't warm yourself by last night's fire, however brightly it may blaze in your memory. Now it's only a heap of ashes, and if you would be warm, you must build another fire.

Once you have run with the foxes, how can you go back to being a hare again? Better to be the least of foxes than king of the hares. All the happy toys of childhood—the dolls and the lead soldiers—where are they now?

Life never stands still. Life is to be lived. It is to be lived at the level we've come up to. We can't hold on to anything for long. If we do, we'll wish we'd let it go. We can't even hold on to a breath; we have to let it go in order to breathe again.

Change

I have resisted change with all my will,
cried out to life, "Pass by and leave me still."
But I have found as I have trudged time's track
that all my wishing will not hold life back.
All finite things must go their finite way;
I cannot bid the merest moment, "Stay."
So finding that I have no power to change
change, I have changed myself. And this is strange,
but I have found out when I let change come,
the very change that I was fleeing from
has often held the good I had prayed for,
and I was not the less for change, but more.
Once I accepted life and was not loath
to change, I found change was the seed of growth.

Pete Rhea, Jim's stepson, turns four.

And Not a Sound Was Heard

I sat and looked at the mountain and I laughed.
I laughed not because the mountain was there
but because I was there.
I laughed to be alive—
and what am I alive for if not to laugh?

I said to the mountain,
"I believe I have the right to address you, sir.
Princes can speak to mountains,
and poets are at least the equal of princes."
Then I heard the mountain laughing.
I wondered,
is this mountain laughing at me or with me?

Suddenly I sensed
that the trees were laughing too,
and the streams and the grass and the rocks
and the earth under my feet;
we laughed—they and I—
there upon the laughing mountain,
rocking through space together,
rolling with the laughter of being!

If You Reach

The stars crowd close around me when I walk
at night sometimes. Like swarms of summer flies
circling my head, they dance before my eyes—
would dart into my mouth if I dared talk.
To keep the stars from catching in my hair,
I try to brush them from me, but my hands
get tangled with the light as in the strands
  the little spiders spin upon the air.
Some learned people think that stars are far
away, but they seem close to me as sight—
friendly and warm and near as candlelight;
  I feel a kindly kinship with a star.
  Light-years are for astronomers; I teach
that you can touch the heavens if you reach.

A Fish Not Even Gold

A few years ago in my garden I built two shallow lily ponds and put goldfish into them. They multiplied. But dogs tore the liner and ruined the ponds, so in the fall I drained them and gave away the fish.

Later that fall, much rain fell, and in the winter, much snow. Two or three inches of water formed in the bottom of the pools. It must have been frozen solid for at least a month and must have frozen solid and thawed a number of times. There may have been times when the pools were dry.

When spring came, I went out one Sunday afternoon to measure the pools, because I intended to rebuild them. I measured the larger pool, then went to the smaller one. It had no water in it. It had rained a week before, so how long it had been dry I do not know. There were a few spots of half-dry, oozy muck in the bottom.

On top of this muck, in the sun, on its side and not breathing, lay a goldfish about three inches long.

I still remember my surprise at seeing it, there in the middle of that empty pond, shining in the sun, a little red-gold fish. It has to be dead, I thought. But almost as I thought it, something in that fish said: "No, no, I am alive. Pick me up."

I ran to the house and got a glass of water.

I picked up the fish—and it gasped!

I put it in the glass, and for a long time it did not move again. I could see that one fin was gone and part of its side was damaged.

I moved the fish from the glass into a larger bowl. For several days, it showed almost no sign of life, but little by little its vitality came back, and in a week, that little fish was lashing with life. That fish was the most alive creature I ever saw. It spent every waking moment flashing, darting, hurtling around that bowl and trying to push through the glass.

When I put it back into the lily pond, it lived in the pond as if to know how dear life is and was not going to waste a moment of it.

How had it survived that winter of freezing and thawing and

drying out? It is hard to surmise.

And what if I had not gone out to the pond on that March day? A few more minutes at most and it surely would have died.

But it lived—lived to live furiously again!

You may not think so, but I will always believe I had to go out to that pond because it had to live.

I suppose you had to see my fish to understand. You had to pick it up. You had to see it lashing about that bowl. You had to see it whirling through that pond.

Somehow that fish had the livingness of life in it.

What a fuss to make about a fish, you may be saying, and a ridiculous coincidence!

I am only such a fish, not even gold. And my pond is also a perilous, precarious place; it, too, has had many times of freezing, of thawing, and of drying out.

And like my fish, I, too, am here, I feel, because I have called, and the feet of the world have been no less swift when they ran to succor me.

We are all linked, one to another. We answer, though we have heard no voice. We respond, though we do not know we have been summoned.

And the universe responds to us—with powers you could not think were there, by ways you had no forethought of, bringing help you could not know would come.

To Thine Own Self

The lake looked at the mountain, and thought:
O fortunate mountain, rising so high,
while I must lie so low.
You look far out across the world
and take part in many interesting happenings,
while I can only lie still.
How I wish I were a mountain!

The mountain looked at the lake, and thought:
O fortunate lake, lying so close
to the warm-breasted Earth
while I loom here
craggy, cold, and uncomfortable.
You are always so peaceful,
while I am constantly having to battle
howling storm and blazing sun.
How I wish I were a lake!

All the time, quietly,
the mountain was coming down
in silver streams to run into the lake,
and the lake was rising as silver mists
to fall as snow upon the mountain.

Rivers Hardly Ever

Rivers hardly ever run in a straight line.
Rivers are willing to take ten thousand meanders
and enjoy every one
and grow from every one—
when they leave a meander,
they are always more
than when they entered it.
When rivers meet an obstacle,
they do not try to run over it;
they merely go around,
but they always get to the other side.
Rivers accept things as they are,
conform to the shape they find the world in—
yet nothing changes things more than rivers;
rivers move even mountains into the sea.
Rivers hardly ever are in a hurry,
yet is there anything more likely
to reach the point it sets out for
than a river?

Live Young!

Ah, to be young forever! How people have longed for that.

The fountain of youth! The elixir of life! The philosopher's stone!

Surely somewhere—in the guarded fruit of a forbidden tree, the enchanted waters of a lost well, a secret formula, an occult incantation, the touch of a sorcerer's wand, the creams and potions from a beautician's vat—there is something to free us from the tyranny of time and keep us young forever!

It is an ancient dream.

Today we are voyaging in space. One of the dreams of the space age is that as we move at rocket speeds time will but slowly gain upon us. We may be able to move through time as through space, even go backward and become children again.

Time! One of the dimensions in which we live! It winds forward and backward from the present like a scroll, but as it is unrolled before us it is rewound behind us so that no more than one line is ever visible.

Space seems like a room where we can look around us. But time is like an aperture through which we peer at a peep show.

Today scientists write about space-time and speak of time as if it were the fourth dimension. Time is not the fourth dimension. Time is the cross section of the fourth dimension. It is the only way we three-dimensional creatures can experience the fourth dimension.

Eternity is the fourth dimension. Time and eternity are related as a point is related to a plane or a plane to a cube, if you can remember your geometry. Time is a plane of the cube of eternity. We can see time, but we cannot see eternity.

Now we read the scroll a line at a time. But the scroll is not a line at a time. It is entire—to be grasped at a glance, had we the vision!

To rise beyond the plane of consciousness in which we are caught and see eternity whole—surely this is the true meaning of immortality. This is the nirvana of Buddhists, the samadhi of Hindus, the heaven of Christians.

The fountain of youth! The elixir of life!
The philosopher's stone!
Surely somewhere—in the guarded fruit of a forbidden tree, the enchanted waters of a lost well, a secret formula, an occult incantation, the touch of a sorcerer's wand, the creams and potions from a beautician's vat—there is something to free us from the tyranny of time and keep us young forever!

It is an ancient dream.

" 'I am the Alpha and the Omega,' says the Lord God, who is and who was and who is to come, the Almighty" (Rev. 1:8).

"Jesus said … 'before Abraham was, I am.' " (Jn. 8:58).

He also said, "Unless you change and become like children, you will never enter the kingdom of heaven" (Mt. 18:3).

Surely, he was telling us that in order to be immortal, we must be immortally young. We must have the spirit and the mind of youth.

What is youth?

Part of being young, certainly, is to believe in immortality. No one ever altogether believes he can cease to exist; but when we are young, we are certain that we have forever. Time is no concern; we have our pockets full of it. We spend it like a prodigal or give it away. The hours stretch out before us endlessly. We may fill them furiously with hubbub or the hardest work, or we may spend a summer lounging under a tree but living in the clouds.

When we are young, the most earthbound of us spends part of his time in the clouds. For youth is imagination, a time of quests and questionings, a time when people dream higher than they ever will again. The young are all poets, though they may never scribble a line. Their thoughts are poetry, for they think in dreams. The logic of dreams is not of the mind but the heart.

So the young confound their elders, who want them to be reasonable. But because they are not lost in old facts, they sometimes find new truths.

The young are always venturing beyond the ends of the Earth—and not falling off. And only those who dare the deep can scale the height. The young may fall off cliffs but also scale mountains. They may occasionally have wrecks but also set new records.

The generations do outstrip one another.

Would you be young?

What are you doing to outstrip yourself and your contemporaries?

Youth is faith. You cannot be bound by facts and be young. Facts are the fences beyond which knowledge has not yet extended. Someone young is always pushing through the fence and enlarging the clearing.

The young annoy their elders by paying no attention to the "Keep Off the Impossible" signs with which age has littered the place. It could only be a man young and free enough to walk on air who would dare to walk on water.

The young have faith in God within. They feel God stirring. God is imprisoned, but He will stand free.

The young are rebels, divine rebels, indignant at the iniquities and inequities of the world, refusing to submit to the ukases and usages of age.

The young are incomplete, but they have the passion for perfection. This is the keenness of youth. They are the bow of longing fitted with the arrows of desire, bent to the full by the Archer of Life. Youth is a zest for the best.

To the young, forever is a moment and a moment is forever, and they give themselves to living it.

Youth is not a time of life but a time of being alive. When we are young, we never walk if we can run, and we can dance all night—and do, in our thoughts at least. Oh, the dancing thoughts of youth, playing leapfrog with the ways of the fathers, turning cartwheels through ancient complacencies!

To be young is to be full of vigor. This is what we really want when we say we want to be young again. We want to live at full vigor.

Vigor has little to do with age, as youth has little to do with years. Vigor is possible at any age. Some men and women have more vigor at sixty than at twenty and can still outwork, outwalk, outdream, and outthink most striplings.

Vigor and youth are not gifts vouchsafed us at any age. We win them by being vigorous and youthful. Some are never vigorously young. Some are youthfully vigorous always.

life

In this world where scientists tell us there are no absolutes, is anything more relative than age?

How old was Albert Einstein at seventy? How old was Thomas Edison at eighty? How old was Charles Fillmore at ninety? How old was Pablo Picasso? How old was Robert Frost?

Not long ago a lass of eighty-eight wrote to me, "I am looking forward to old age."

A rose-cheeked, straight-limbed lad of ninety-five laughed when his children introduced us and said: "Don't believe them. They are lying to you. I am not their father. I am their brother."

Time cannot wither a vital spirit. Age cannot dry up the spring of mind. It is only when we lose faith in our power to grow and settle comfortably down that we begin to be old.

Age complains of youth, "Will it never settle down?" But youth knows that life cannot settle down. Life is a sea voyage. On a sea voyage, to settle down is to sink.

The young do not know what lies ahead. Their powers are untried. They have not found themselves and their meaning.

But which of us has found ourselves and our meaning? You may have made some island port of commonsensible contentment, but is this the port you started for? Is this all you hoped to become? Can you remember the dreams of your youth?

The young know that they have not arrived. But no one has arrived. There is not one area of life where we can say, "All has been done that can be done!" The horizon stretches endlessly in all directions. Youth is the jubilant conviction that yet more is to be found—in you and in the world.

Youth is the power to grow. This is the definition of youth.

Stone lasts for centuries by slowing down its processes of change. Yet even the hardest stone must at last disintegrate in the wild dance of its atoms; its stone-stuff will become the roots and leaves of plants, the bone and blood of beasts.

But life is not like stone.

On a warm summer night, corn grows so fast you can hear it grow. On a sunny afternoon, a muddy-colored wriggler crawls out of a pond, fastens itself to a stem of grass, and while we watch, emerges from its shriveled skin to soar on wings that were not there an hour before—a green-gold dragonfly.

A living thing is like a piece

of music. It is not enough to listen to the opening bars or closing chords. You have to hear it played clear through.

You cannot truly take the picture of a living thing. It changes as the shutter clicks.

Will the caterpillar tell you of the butterfly? Or the bullfrog of the polliwog? And how will you know the man? By the babe, or the boy, or the stripling, or the father of the family, or the gray beard?

To live is to change. Nothing alive stands still. A tree may rest in winter but only to gather strength to grow again in spring.

Life is like fire.

In the heart of every living cell, there is a fire. In the heart of everyone alive, there is a fire.

Fire is change. It never stays the same two seconds together. It lives only by growing. What it touches, it consumes; but what it consumes, it transforms.

When it touches a dead branch, the branch is consumed and transformed! The dead branch becomes dancing flame.

So it is with life. When life kindles inanimate clay, clay can lie still no longer. It has to move and grow and turn into a trout or a bird or a tree or a bit of moss or a human being. It becomes alive.

We cannot live like stone. We must live like fire that lives by growing.

This is the secret of the never-flagging, everlasting vigor of the sun. The sun turns its very atom-stuff into fire and quickens the world around it into life.

On a warm summer night, corn grows so fast you can hear it grow. On a sunny afternoon, a muddy-colored wriggler crawls out of a pond, fastens itself to a stem of grass, and while we watch, emerges from its shriveled skin to soar on wings that were not there an hour before—a green-gold dragonfly.

O God, I pray You, let me like a living sun catch fire with love and burn with Truth, igniting all I ever touch with the same love of Truth that I have!

Of all Earth's living things, trees have the longest span of life. And of all living things, they have the longest span of growth. If they live a thousand years, they grow a thousand years. Trees never cease to grow.

To live is to grow.

If we human beings would lengthen the time of our lives, we must lengthen the time of our growth.

You may think there is a limit to the growth you can make.

This may be true of your body. But you are more mind than body,

and you are more spirit than mind. In mind and spirit, who dares set a limit on the growth one may make?

A redwood is tall, taking thousands of years to reach its full height. Are you less than a redwood?

Has God not said He created us in His image? How tall is the image of God?

What dimensions has your mind? What span has your spirit?

Are you grown up in your God-likeness?

Oh, what everlasting livingness lies all about us and within us yet to be attained! We are spiritual striplings.

We are children of God.
Youth is the power to grow.
To grow is to be alive.
Would you be alive?
Then live young!

Will the caterpillar tell you of the butterfly? Or the bullfrog of the polliwog?

And Beauty Too!

Flowers are so beautiful—I see
no reason why they have to be;
considered practically, would
not ugly flowers have been as good?
But something more than good enough
is elemental in the stuff
of things, a joyous, upward twist
that draws a rainbow from a mist;
that gives a lizard feathered wings
and makes of it a bird that sings;
that chooses an unlikely beast,
not swift or strong—one of the least—
and calls forth in it man who may
climb clear to Christlikeness some day!

My Heart Makes Its Own Weather

My heart makes its own weather,
so let the world grow gray;
my heart starts saying April
when April's far away.

In spite of rain and reason
and winter on the wing,
my heart has its own season,
and my heart says it is spring!

Blow wind and bitter weather,
come care and whistling cold,
an April heart will never
grow gray or crabbed or old.

Time is a wrinkled treason;
age is an old untruth.
Heart, keep your changeless season,
green April, golden youth!

The Cherry Tree

When I first moved into the place where I now live, growing outside my window was a cherry tree—aged, stunted, twisted, black.

One stormy night this miserable little tree broke off at the ground. When I examined the stump, I found it crawling with termites.

So I hacked the stump back into the ground and poured creosote over and through and around the remains.

I then forgot the tree. But when spring came, up from that mutilated, tortured stump a twig appeared, and the twig grew into a stem, and the stem put forth branches and leaves.

I asked a nurseryman if he thought there was any chance that the thing would live and bear fruit.

"None at all," he said. "It is valueless. Chop it down."

But I did not chop it down.

That has now been many years. The little tree did not die. It grew.

All the years I have lived here, I have picked cherries from it—red, delicious, perfect cherries—at least enough for a pie or two.

If it were an orchard of cherry trees, it could not give so much to me; for the little tree glows life-colored in my heart, and even more than cherries, I have gathered courage from it.

"Life is stronger than death," says the tree. "Whatever appearances may be, never accept them."

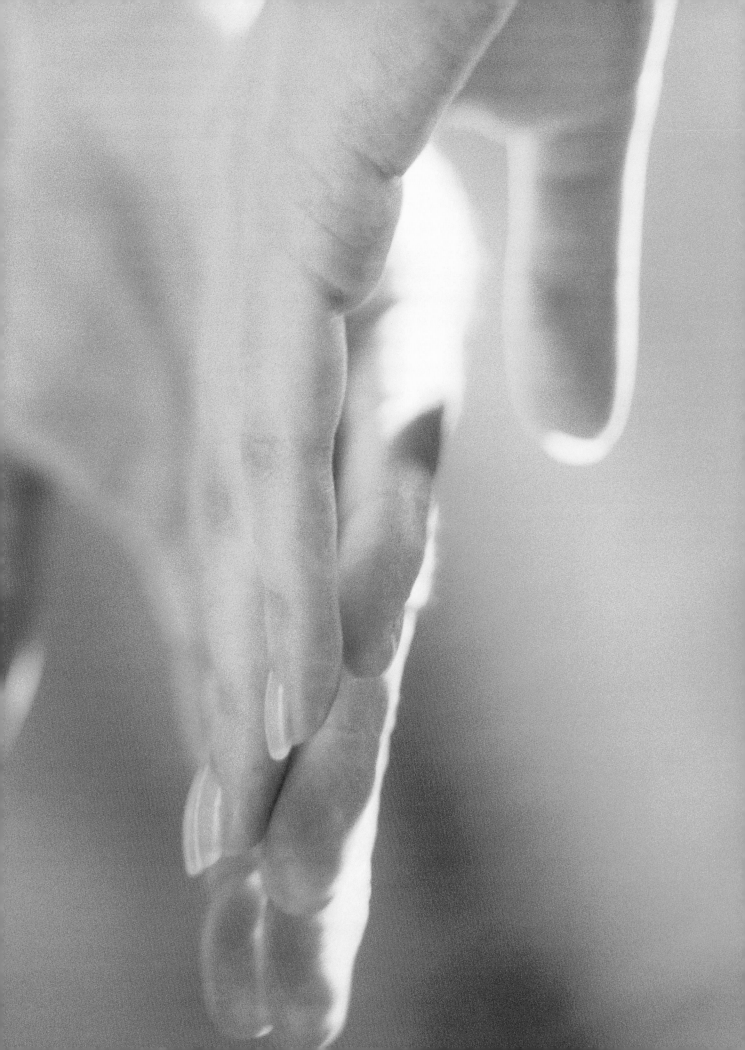

VI.

Love

Wisdom

The wise and learned sage
on the pretentious page
writes: "In two words defined,
God is divine mind."

But infants' helpless wiles,
mere cockleshells of smiles,
say without words or art,
"God is the human heart."

When We Look With Eyes of Love

There is so much more to all of us than the obvious.

A few times in my life I have gotten a glimpse of the real Self of a person. It was only for an anguished moment and only because I looked with eyes of love.

But for an anguished moment, I looked with eyes of love and I saw. I cannot say what I saw, but I knew that it was something inexpressibly beautiful. I shall always believe I was looking at being as it really is, and I saw beauty naked.

I believe that is what I would see if I saw the real Self of you. But I have to look with eyes of love.

That is why lovers go around starry-eyed. They have seen through what is form to what is real, and it has left them dazzled. They can only murmur, "Beautiful."

We look at what they are looking at and wonder how they can see so much in such a plain creature. But it is our vision that is imperfect.

Love raises vision to a higher power that eye charts cannot measure.

Billie and Jim Freeman.

Love's Omnipotence

Sometimes I think how little I know me.
I am the unexplored, for the most part;
I stand, as it were, on the edge of a wide sea,
and the sea I gaze upon is my own heart.

For I have other dimensions and am more
than I have judged I was from surface seeing;
this face, this body—these are but the shore;
how far beyond them stretch my seas of being!

I have thought I was an island, a rocky shelf
of separateness, but the eternal deep
forever breaks across my reefs of self.
In me and over me and through me sweep

the seas of God, and often now I sense
that I am one with love's omnipotence.

She Lets Us Love Her

Just to be loving.
Just to be loved.
How few of us know
that is enough!

My dog is very much a dog;
she does nothing
except what a dog should do,
which is largely nothing.
She is not even an especially
affectionate dog—
she does not leap on us
when we come home
or cover us with wet kisses;
but in a quiet way,
like some human beings,
she shows us that she loves us.

She is a beautiful dog,
though not even that in
    everyone's eyes.
But she does none of the things
we human beings have come to
    feel are necessary:
she does not possess a fortune;
she does no useful work;
she has no fame or important
    position in the community;
she shows no exceptional talent.

She does no great feats
so that we can brag about her to
    the neighbors.
She does not even guard the
    house
or do clever tricks for company.

She does only one thing—
she lets us love her.
No more than this,
but this is enough.

She needs no other reason for
    being
except to let us love her.
Love justifies all the expense
    and care
we lavish on her
and compensates us for
    the nuisance
she sometimes is,
like every living thing.

Just to be loved.
Just to be loving.
This is reason enough for being.
Have you ever thought of that?

You there pursuing so intently

all those grand schemes
and lofty ambitions
you feel you have to pursue
in order to be of value—
you there striving so hard—
for what?
My dog lets me love her—
no more than this—
and that is reason enough—
and more—
for her to be.

How glad I am
that we found her
and have her living with us.
My wife and I are willing to be
her maid and cook and nurse and
companion and provider.

There she lies,
stretched out indolently on
        the floor,
and she lets me pet her,
if I will take the trouble to bend
down.

I look at her
and I know something
more about life
than I knew without her.
I know what is necessary
        and important—
and what is not.

Jim and Zahd.

The Heart Will Find Its Own

How sweet are the syllables that signify love! Heart has no deeper longing than to utter or hear uttered the words "I love you!" They are like the sight of land to a sailor long adrift.

We pursue many ends—power and pleasure, riches and knowledge, health and fame—and they are worthy ends, but without love they are little more than a child's toys.

Without love this existence is life imprisonment. Until love sets us free, each of us is confined in the narrow prison of himself. Who has never felt that he is bound as by walls? Love bursts these walls of self and selfishness.

We seek and do not know what it is that we seek. Yet often a word would fill the emptiness, a touch would ease the ache. How little of love it takes to make a house of happiness out of a lonely heart!

We have seen love: in the look of a young man and woman, in the fingers of a mother fondling her baby, in the clasped hands of friends, in the bent back of an old priest bowed in the service of God, in the eyes of a student poring over treasured volumes, in the faces of soldiers marching in the ranks of hate, in the patience of a biologist peering through his microscope, in the beauty and order of the universe that are the signs of God's love for us.

What is love?

To understand love, as to understand God, one must experience it. Some seek popularity believing that this approval of people in general is love, but love is more than popularity. Others seek prestige believing that this is love, but love is more than prestige.

For above all, love is a sharing. Love is a power. Love is a change that takes place in our own heart. Sometimes it may change others, but always it changes us.

To love is to find happiness in making others happy. It is to understand what others think and feel and need. It is to say and do the things that make them eager to be with us and to do these things not for effect but because it is natural for us to do them.

It is to know the imperfections of others yet see them perfect.

It is to know their weaknesses yet see them strong, and because of our vision and our faith to make them stronger than they are.

It is to accept others as they are and when they fail our aspirations for them or spurn our outstretched hand, to keep open the door of our heart.

It is to appreciate the importance of others and to help them appreciate their own importance.

It is to grow into the heart of others and to become a part of their life yet not bind their heart nor limit their life.

It is to lose ourself in something greater than ourself, as a small spark loses itself in other sparks and becomes a star.

There is no unworthy love. The object of love may be unworthy. But love is the supreme beauty, the final joy. Even if sorrow comes with love, love makes us able to meet it and transfigure it, to rise through it as we could not have done had we never loved.

When we are in love—with an idea, a person, people, God—we walk upon the pinnacles of life. We are lifted out of ourselves and become something more than we have ever been before.

Some are afraid to love, afraid lest their love be unreturned, afraid lest someone catch a glimpse behind their careful mask. It is true

that love will lift the mask—but how gentle are the eyes of love! To be afraid to love is to be afraid to live.

Some say that they love God but not humanity. But how can we love harmony and not music? How can we love light and not the morning? How can we love nature and not the spring? How can we love God and not the likeness of God, which we are?

When some feel that they have love, they have only a word. It is easy to say that we love strangers when they are far from us or that we love God when God is but a shadowy abstraction. But when the stranger knocks at our heart and cries, "Share!"—when God becomes the disturber in our soul who answers, "Serve!"—then we find out if we truly love.

Some want to love but do not know how. They are like children who wish to make music but have not mastered any instrument. They have not learned, but one can learn to love. The beginning of love is giving.

For those who have never given, it is not easy to give. Let them begin by giving but a little. Let them give a smile where they would have passed unheeding. Let them give a kind word where they

Some say that they love God but not humanity. But how can we love harmony and not music? How can we love light and not the morning? How can we love nature and not the spring? How can we love God and not the likeness of God, which we are?

would not have spoken.

If you will take one faltering step, love will rush to meet you and bear you on. For love is the great giver.

Do you wish to find yourself? You must lose yourself. Do you wish to be the master of life? You must be its servant. Do you wish to receive love? You must give it.

Receiving is a pleasure, but giving is life itself. It is only by giving self away that a person grows.

The mind that withholds its wisdom, the strength that refuses the burden is like a wasteland, sterile and meaningless. It is not because it never receives fresh supplies of water but because it has no outlet that the Dead Sea is dead. If the Sun should stop giving its light, it would become only another dead star.

We may be a chaos or a cosmos. We may succumb to hate and death or rise to love and life. Love is mightier than hate. Life is stronger than death. To learn to love is to learn the secret of life.

There is a power that links the Earth and Sun and binds the stars together into galaxies, a power that binds the segments of life into a perfect whole. Alone in our little self, we feel our incompleteness. We know in our heart that we are a part of something more.

Love is the power that links

the lonely islands of men's souls, beaten by icy separating seas of ignorance and fear and circumstance. Love is the power that links us all in God, as all the islands are linked in the Earth. Yet love is not a chain. Love is completion.

The river runs into the sea, and its waters mingle with the waters of the sea. The sea is not the river and the river is not the sea. Yet who can separate one from the other?

O God of love, You are the sea and we are a river flowing to the sea! Who shall say which is the river and which is the sea?

You are a flame and we are steel tempered in the flame. Who shall say which is the steel and which is the flame?

You are fulfillment and we are desire. Who shall say which is the desire and which is the fulfillment?

You are spirit and we are flesh. Who shall say which is the flesh and which is the spirit?

For this is the mystery and miracle of love, that we are separate yet we are one! And the heart, though it must overleap eternity, will find its own.

We have seen love: in the look of a young man and woman, in the fingers of a mother fondling her baby, in the clasped hands of friends, in the bent back of an old priest bowed in the service of God … in the beauty and order of the universe that are the

signs of God's love for us.

love

I the Human Being Come With My Human Heart

Love is not passion,
but love that has no passion in it
is not love.
It is no more love
than an artificial rose made in
    Hong Kong
is a live and fragrant bloom.

Love is a fire,
and fire, I have observed,
does not inquire politely of
    the fagots,
"Do you wish to burn?"
Love may not stand
and knock at the door
on a windless summer night
and beg you to come down
and let her in.

Love, and you may find yourself
rising from your bed at night
to wander down strange ways
that you did not even know
    were there
and where you had no wish to go,
asking all whom you meet,
"Have you seen him whom I love?"

And when you find him,
you will not be able to let him go
but will follow him
wherever he may take you,
not because he bids you come,
but out of love's necessities
at the bidding of your own heart.
Love is not a sentimental journey,
love is a passionate pursuit.

When I love,
I the housewife
come warm to my husband's desires.
I the husband
come gentle to my wife's needs.
I the mother and father
come with reassurance when my
    children question and demand.
I the nurse
come with patience to my patients.
I the teacher
come on fire to teach even when my
    students have no wish to learn.
I the worker
come running to my rendezvous
    with work.
I the human being

92

come with my human heart
to comfort the human sorrow
and bind up the human pain.
I the man of God
come with no thought of self to do
      Compassion's will.

Love is not an intellectual thing
or a matter of fulfilling the
      requirements—
the soldier snapping to attention
or the worker punching the
      time clock.
Love entwines the lover and the
      loved one,
the soldier and his duty,
and the worker and his work,
in such a tangled net of
      consciousness
that no one can be sure
whether one answers because he
      hears the other
call in need,
or whether one calls because he
      hears the other's
need to answer.

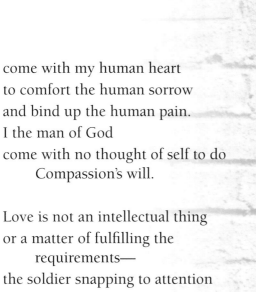

What Hand Did You Expect Him to Use?

Love is not something
showered down on us like rain
out of the heavens.
The only love I have ever run into
has always begun in someone's human heart.

If I cannot love those whom it is easy to love—
my wife, my mother, my sister, my child—
how will I love those whom it is hard to love?
If I don't love what it is natural to love,
will I love what is supernatural?
God Himself has told us that those who say
they love God whom they have not seen
and do not love those close and dear to them
whom they have seen—
they are liars.
The love that is God is first of all
the love that is human.

A woman in desperate need
went into a church to pray.
She cried out:
"God, if there is a God,
let me become aware of Your presence.
I need to feel you as
a real loving help in my life."
Just then she felt a hand brush her shoulder.

She burst into tears of joy and sprang up.
When she turned around, a friend
was standing behind her.
"I was praying to God
to come to me," she said,
"and I thought I felt His hand,
but it was yours, wasn't it?"
Her friend looked at her gently for a moment.
"What hand did you expect Him to use," she said,
"but the hand that was closest to you!"

If God is love,
must it not be true
that human love is divine
and divine love is human?
If God is love,
is there any love that is not divine?

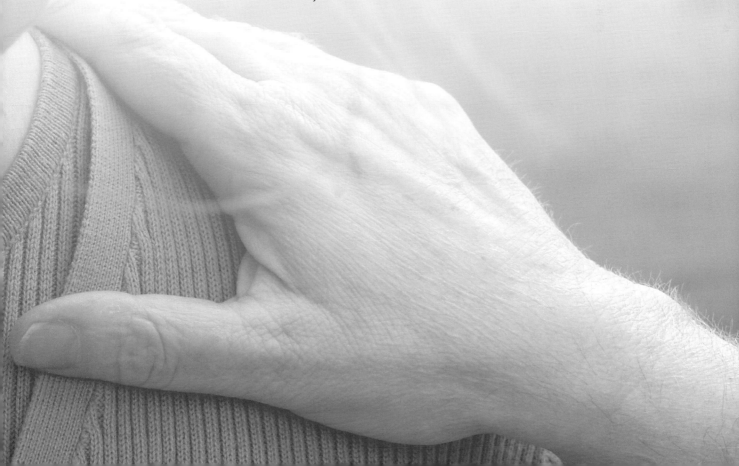

Blessing for a Marriage

May your marriage bring you all the exquisite excitements a marriage
  should bring,
    and may life grant you also patience, tolerance, and understanding.
May you always need one another—
not so much to fill your emptiness as to help you to know your fullness.
A mountain needs a valley to be complete;
    the valley does not make the mountain less, but more;
and the valley is more a valley because it has a mountain towering
  over it.
So let it be with you and you.
May you need one another, but not out of weakness.
May you want one another, but not out of lack.
May you entice one another, but not compel one another.
May you embrace one another, but not encircle one another.
May you succeed in all important ways with one another,
    and not fail in the little graces.
May you look for things to praise, often say, "I love you!"
    and take no notice of small faults.
If you have quarrels that push you apart,
May both of you hope to have good sense enough to take the first
  step back.
May you enter into the mystery which is the awareness of one another's
    presence—
no more physical than spiritual, warm and near when you are side
  by side,
and warm and near when you are in separate rooms or even distant cities.

May you have happiness, and may you find it making one
   another happy.
May you have love, and may you find it loving one another!

   Thank You, God,
   for Your presence here with us
   and Your blessing on this marriage.
   Amen.

Jim and Katherine's wedding picture.

A Praise of Sex and Love

Surely God meant sexual love
to be a psalm of joy-in-life,
a song to celebrate
our body's power to give and take delight.
It is a song no one has to teach us to sing—
the music is written in our cells.

Full of grace notes and pleasant surprises,
it may be sung in several different keys,
but it is most beautiful
when the dominant note is trust
and the song begins and ends on the tonic chord
of mutual respect and understanding.

It is not a choral number,
God wrote it as a two-part song.
When two sing happily together
and practice till they grow familiar with the tune
and one another's change of pace and variance of style,
then hidden overtones and harmonies emerge,
at once intense and delicate,
small heightenings of sound too subtle to be written down,
but the Composer hoped the singers
would discover and draw them forth.

Then the song becomes what God meant it to be,
rising tuneful note by note
through dolce and crescendo
to a glorious hallelujah,
thence subsiding at the end
into a great amen of peace.

VII.

Grief

I had gone to pray for Katherine in the Silent Unity prayer room at 917 Tracy in Kansas City. As I sat there in agony, unable to bring my mind into enough order to speak words of prayer, suddenly I heard a voice. The voice was so real, so audible that I looked around to see who was there. The voice said: "Do you need Me? I am there." As I sat there, the voice continued.

I Am There

Do you need Me?
I am there.
You cannot see Me, yet I am the light you see by.
You cannot hear Me, yet I speak through your voice.
You cannot feel Me, yet I am the power at work in your hands.
I am at work, though you do not understand My ways.
I am at work, though you do not recognize My works.
I am not strange visions. I am not mysteries.
Only in absolute stillness, beyond self, can you know Me as I am, and
then but as a feeling and a faith.
Yet I am there. Yet I hear. Yet I answer.
When you need Me, I am there.
Even if you deny Me, I am there.
Even when you feel most alone, I am there.
Even in your fears, I am there.
Even in your pain, I am there.
I am there when you pray and when you do not pray.
I am in you, and you are in Me.
Only in your mind can you feel separate from Me, for only in your mind
are the mists of "yours" and "mine."
Yet only with your mind can you know Me and experience Me.
Empty your heart of empty fears.

When you get yourself out of the way, I am there.

You can of yourself do nothing, but I can do all.

And I am in all.

Though you may not see the good, good is there, for I am there.

I am there because I have to be, because I am.

Only in Me does the world have meaning; only out of Me does the world take form; only because of Me does the world go forward.

I am the law on which the movement of the stars and the growth of living cells are founded.

I am the love that is the law's fulfilling.

I am assurance.

I am peace.

I am oneness.

I am the law that you can live by.

I am the love that you can cling to.

I am your assurance.

I am your peace.

I am one with you.

I am.

Though you fail to find Me, I do not fail you.

Though your faith in Me is unsure, My faith in you never wavers, because I know you, because I love you.

Beloved, I am there.

This Is My Gift

This is my gift—
to find the world a wilderness
and leave it a garden,
to come into a wasteland
and build in it
a city
full of towers and conversations
and music and visions and
shining deeds …
to lift up the Earth to be a star
in a world of stars.

Still the Glory Is Not Gone

One night I lay down by my wife
so tired that I was tired of life,
so close to love, so close to death
I lay, almost too close for breath.

There from the midnight cliffs of mind,
leaving all things and thought behind,
I looked at everything on Earth
and saw what everything is worth.
I saw then what life's meanings are,
what I am doing on this star,
citizen of the universe,
meeting the better and the worse,
whether willing or whether loath,
for the law of life is the law of growth.
I saw the secret in the seed,
saw the lily in the weed,
saw life in death, saw in the tomb
only the resurrecting womb!
I looked at life and saw it plain,
and saw the meaning of the pain,

Saw heaven's rim, though it was hell,
and though I had no words to tell
what I had seen, I understood—
saw through the pain and saw it good!
And knew that somehow I am part
of being, heart of the inmost heart!

Then through my hell of helplessness,
I felt an unseen presence press,
and when I rose it lingered on,
and still the glory is not gone.

A Step Back Toward Life

When I woke on that first Christmas morning of aloneness, I did not want to get out of bed. I had planned to be away on Christmas and had taken a trip to California, with the thought that I might stay there, but I had soon realized I was more alone in California than I was here in Missouri—living in my familiar apartment, doing my familiar work, meeting my familiar friends—so I had to come back.

I did not want to wake at all; if I could have slept through that Christmas, I believe I would have done so. But wake I did, and at my usual early hour; it was not even daylight yet.

As a child, I had learned to be an early riser. My grandfather had taught me that.

My grandfather had taught me many things. When I was a small boy, he and I would always be up hours before dawn, down in the kitchen, lighting the coal stove, where he would fix us heaping plates of potatoes and eggs. And on Christmas morning I would come creeping through the dark from my room into his. While he went downstairs "to see if Santa Claus has gotten here," I would lie impatiently in his huge feather bed; or more likely, I would leap up and down in its voluptuous billows, my mind a torrent and torment of imagination, and my body, often literally, at a fever pitch of anticipation, as I waited to hear his voice: "All right, Jim, you can come down. I believe Santa Claus has been here." Then I would make a headlong plunge down the stairs into the parlor.

My grandfather had taught me to read and write long before I had started to school. He had taught me out of fairytale books and history books, out of the Bible and books of poems. He loved Poe, so he cajoled and bribed me into memorizing "Annabel Lee," which I would recite for his friends for a penny.

As I lay there that Christmas morning, I wondered if that had been prophetic.

But lying in bed thinking back to earlier and happier Christmases was not going to help me to live through this one. My childhood and my grandfather were gone many years before.

And so was my wife—Katherine had died three months before.

Lying here thinking would not bring her back. All my thoughts— and all my prayers!—had not kept her alive.

I could not comprehend how such a thing could happen. Why should she have died? She must have asked why too, in the silence of her own soul, where none could hear her cry. But one thing she had showed me clearly, as I had kept watch beside her and shared her pain: Through prayer and faith and love, you can come to a place in your soul where the most that life can do to you is make you say, "Ouch!" and eventually it cannot even do *that*.

I still cannot understand how Love—and if there is a God, He *must* be Love—can make a world with so much pain and death; probably I never will. Half the things I have written have been my search for answers. I am sure my poems are part of my search.

How can I convey to you what, perhaps, the mind has no power to reach? What is the secret, silent wisdom of the heart? I only know that it is possible to catch a glimpse of things, not as we ordinarily experience them, but in another dimension—as from eternity?—and, in this larger frame, see that it is possible to have faith. Even when all visible support for faith is swept away, life and its events, however puzzling they may now seem to be, make sense and have meaning, and that meaning is good.

But I have gotten away from my story. I had to get out of bed and get through a day I dreaded to meet, Christmas without the one I love.

I still cannot understand how Love—and if there is a God, He *must* be Love—can make a world with so much pain and death; probably I never will. Half the things I have written have been my search for answers. I am sure my poems are part of my search.

Christmas had meant so much to both of us. I remembered our first Christmas—before we were married; we had been going together about a year. The day I came to work in Silent Unity, we had started going together. She stopped me on that first day as I came through the office and told me that a group of fellows and girls were going to spend the weekend together. The fellows had rented one cottage, and the girls had rented another. Would I like to go? She had a car and would be glad to take me. By the time we went back to work on Monday, we were in love.

I pushed away the pillow that lay alongside me. Since she had died, I had slept with an extra pillow. I told myself it was to help me go to sleep, but I knew the pillow was more than that: for fourteen years I had slept beside my wife.

Slowly I swung my legs over the side of the bed and sat there in the dark. I was glad it was dark. In the dark, I could not see how empty the room was.

The clock in the hall struck the hour. I counted the chimes: one, two, three, four, five, six. I loved that chiming clock; when I woke in the dark alone and heard it ringing out the hour, it gave me

a sense of my whereabouts. It was a beautiful old banjo clock. Katherine and I had anguished over buying it, whether we could spend that much money.

I was glad we had; I needed things like the clock that helped me to locate myself at the center of myself. That was why I had not moved out of the house our apartment was in. When she died, my first thought was to run away, the house was so full of her.

I could not come into a room without her being in the room too. I could not sit in a chair without becoming aware that the empty chair beside me was hers. Wherever I turned, there was something that was hers, something that was ours like the clock, except that now there was no ours, there was only mine.

The apartment, its familiar rooms and objects, was a stabilizing element in my life. Here I was at home. This was a central location not only on the street but also in my soul.

We had lived here four years. We had had a hard time finding this apartment. The war was still on when we had moved in. Before we found it, we had lived in one room in a hotel with paper-thin walls and with neighbors who came home at three in the morn-ing and battled. Only you who lived through the war and know how hard it was to find a decent place to live can appreciate how much that apartment meant to us. It was on the second floor of an old apartment house with only four beautifully spacious apartments in it. It even had a screened-in porch and a pantry. It had a front hall and fireplace in the living room. Not a fireplace where you could burn wood; it had a radiant gas burner with a crinkly asbestos sheet in it but the flames ran sparkling across it, and when we lay in front of it, it spread its warmth through our bodies and glowed in our minds almost as much as a log fire would have. At least it was not hard for us to convince ourselves that this was so. We had loved to lie in front of it. We had a big wool serape we bought in Mexico on a vacation trip, and we would lie on that.

But I was not in Mexico, I was at home, and I probed with my feet until I found my slippers.

I walked into the living room and lit the fireplace. For sev-eral minutes I stood in front of it, watching the sparkling flames, let-ting the heat slowly soak into my face and hands. The heat had not started yet in the radiators.

I had left a record of Christmas carols on the record player, but I did not turn it on. I decided that I was probably the only one awake in the building, and I did not want to waken the others. They are the lucky ones, I thought. Let them sleep.

I wanted to open the presents that were under the tree, but also I didn't want to. As long as I could put off opening them, I would have something to look forward to. I had a good idea what might be in them, that is, all except one.

There was a gift that was a puz-zlement. It was a large box. Three days before Christmas, Katherine's best friend—my friend too, for we had worked together for many years—had brought the box. "You are to take this home," she had told me, "and put it under the tree and not open it until Christmas morning."

"I've bought a tree, but I haven't put it up yet," I said. "You think I ought to?"

"Yes, I do," she said. "If Kath-erine were here, that's what she'd want you to do, isn't that so?"

"She's not here," I said. "May-be I'd be better off if I forgot it was Christmas."

"You can't forget it's Christmas. Christmas always meant too much to Katherine and you. That's why I think you ought to put up your tree and open your presents Christmas morning, just as you always have. And I want you to promise you'll open this gift last of all."

"Why?" I said. "What's in it?"

"If I told you that, it wouldn't be a Christmas present. But yes, I will tell you what's in it. The spirit of Christmas is in it. That's why I want you to open it last. It will carry you triumphantly through the day."

I was glad that she asked me to put up the tree and open my presents Christmas morning, because I wanted to do it. Although I was frightened of what this Christmas would bring, I still wanted Christmas to be Christmas.

Katherine and I had always made a big thing of Christmas and the Christmas tree. We even had decorations that my mother had given me, remnants of my child-

hood. Trimming a tree and rising on Christmas morning to open presents under it seemed almost a rule of life that I could not violate. I suppose it is foolish to build patterns like this into your life, but most of us do.

I went into the kitchen and fixed myself a cup of coffee. That took awhile. I am not a cook. My mother was a good cook and so was my wife. When she became too ill to cook, I had tried feebly to learn, but as long as she could get to the stove, my wife had insisted on cooking for us.

I sat at the kitchen table and slowly drank my coffee. When I finished, I poured another cup and carried it into the dining room.

I had set the Christmas tree on a table in a corner of the dining room. It was not a big tree. I thought as I stood there that it had been foolish of me to decorate it.

There was a gift that was a puzzlement. It was a large box. Three days before Christmas, Katherine's best friend—my friend too, for we had worked together for many years—had brought the box. "You are to take this home," she had told me, "and put it under the tree and not open it until Christmas morning."

110

I turned on the lights on the tree. It was pretty, I thought, and sat for a time staring at it and sipping my coffee. Slowly I became aware that the light was returning to the world outside my window. I walked to the window and looked up and down the street. It was a cloudless sky. It would be clear and cold, I decided. Everything—the leafless trees, the empty yards, the sleeping houses—looked gray and bare in the half light of early morning.

Slowly I opened the presents. I do not remember now what they were. I am sure there was one from my mother; she usually sent me something handmade. And I am sure there was one from a friend named Mark. I was going to have Christmas dinner with him. He had had multiple sclerosis for eight years, and I had become his best friend, at times his only friend; his wife had left him.

I believe there were some other presents, but at last there remained only the box my friend had brought me with instructions that it must be the last gift to open. As I said, it was a puzzlement. I could not guess what she might be giving to me or even why; she had exchanged gifts with my wife but never with me.

The box was neatly wrapped in Christmas paper and had a large bow on it. I have always envied people who can tie bows. When I make them, they turn out to look like blackbirds' nests. I tore off the wrapping and opened the box.

There were three packages in it, all carefully wrapped in silver metallic paper bound in a red bow. It struck me that this had been the way Katherine wrapped her gifts to me. I lifted them out and placed them on the floor. They felt like books. I picked up the first one. There was a small envelope attached to it. On it were a few handwritten words. For an incomprehensible moment, I stared at the handwriting.

I knew that my friend's handwriting resembled Katherine's. But was my friend, or was my mind, playing a strange trick on me? I read the words:

*"To a poet with all my love.
From Katherine"*

I tore open the package. In it was the Cambridge edition of Tennyson's poems. Almost instantly I realized that someone was giving me this because they wanted me to read "In Memoriam," the poem that Tennyson labored and agonized over for seventeen years

grief

There were three packages in it, all carefully wrapped in silver metallic paper bound in a red bow. It struck me that this had been the way Katherine wrapped her gifts to me. I lifted them out and placed them on the floor. They felt like books. I picked up the first one. There was a small envelope attached to it. On it were a few handwritten words. For an incomprehensible moment, I stared at the handwriting.

I knew that my friend's handwriting resembled Katherine's. But was my friend, or was my mind, playing a strange trick on me?

as he searched for faith after the death of his young friend, Arthur Henry Hallam.

Later my friend told me that Katherine had told her how we had seen a replica first edition of "In Memoriam" in a shop that dealt in rare and old books, but when she went to buy it, the book had been sold, and this was the only volume she could find with the complete "In Memoriam" in it.

But I did not stop to think about the book and the poem now. I did not stop to think. I reached for the next package. With trembling hands, I plucked the little card pasted to its top. On it was drawn a small red heart with an arrow through it. I read the card:

"I always wanted you to read this.
Love, Katherine."

For a moment I could not believe what I was reading. I tore open the package. The book was Thomas Mann's *Joseph and His Brothers*. It had just been published that year, but it was not a new book; it was a collection of four of his earlier novels that had been published separately. They were *The Tales of Jacob, Young Joseph, Joseph in Egypt*, and *Joseph the Provider*. Katherine was a constant reader. She had read these

112

novels one by one and told me how much she liked them. But why, out of the myriad books she had read, had she chosen these stories?

At that moment I was incapable of coherent thought, but I have often thought about it since. Was it the story of Jacob and Rachel, which ends with Rachel's death, that she wanted me to read? Her wanting me to read the stories was not, however, a dying thought; long before she had become ill, she had urged me to read them. Did she know, in the strange way we sometimes have of knowing without knowing, that she would be the Rachel to my Jacob? I have often wondered about that. Life is not at all what it mostly seems to be; we are impelled along our outward course by silent inward forces; many things go on in the depths of our souls that never rise to shallow enough levels of our minds for us to catch them with our conscious thinking.

I reached for the third package. There was no card pasted on this. By now I was down on my knees, my hands shaking so hard that I could hardly direct them. With a mighty effort, I tore the paper off the package. Somehow I had expected it to be another book. But it was not a book. It was a red leather

box. I opened the box.

Inside the box there was a narrow shelf on which lay an envelope with two words penciled on it: *"To Jim."*

I lifted out the shelf. In the box were twelve golf balls.

Carefully I took out of the envelope a handwritten letter. There was no question now, this was Katherine's handwriting, these were Katherine's words. As my eyes and my heart stormed through the penciled sentences, I knew that this was Katherine's heart I held in my hands.

My Beloved,

Steady, Jim, steady, dear heart. When you read this, you have survived til Christmas, and the worst is over now.

You and I have dreamed dreams and thought thoughts and been, oh, so close, my dearest. If your heart cannot find the answer to "why, why, why," then for the time being please accept my sure faith and firm trust that all is well with me. For you these may yet be aching hours, and I have felt for you and been greatly concerned, but I have been comforted in this thought: Surely in surrendering you to the law of Love, I have also surrendered you to greater growth, greater understanding, and yes, I am sure, to happiness and joy and fulfillment. Remember to tell me that was so, My Golden One! Never refuse happiness and look with approval and blessing upon it.

You know the way now to the Dwelling of Light, and I am glad, and if ever you are fearful look out in the sky while I no doubt shall be a little Star, how burning bright shall I be in my love for you! I shall keep busy doing my work, waiting until we are together again.

You keep busy with your work, too. V.V.V. You are always in my heart.

Because I have known with you love and passion, and because you brought me beauty and richness in thought and perception of mind and spirit, and because we have watched together firelight and candlelight and sunlight and moonlight, I count myself the most fortunate of women.

I shall bless thee now, and thou shalt forever be a Blessing.

Eternally, in understanding and in Perfect Love,

Your Katherine

Steady, Jim, steady, dear heart, the worst is over now.

I do not know how I managed to read it through, and I will never be sure what happened during those next few minutes.

All I remember now is that when I came to myself, I was stretched out on the floor, and I was weeping as I have never wept before or since. A flood, a storm of sobs was bursting from me, convulsing every inch of my body. I was pounding my chest with my fists. I may have been pounding my head against the floor. My body ached.

But when I stood up and stumbled to the bathroom and washed my face, I suddenly realized, to my astonishment, that my mind was clear and my heart was light.

I have often wondered if it was not the accumulated energy that for many months I had had to gather and hold in, so that I might show the calm spirit I felt I had to show, that must have come cascading out of me in such tumultuous fashion. I do not know whether it was more an expression of anguish or rejoicing, they were so entangled. Undoubtedly it was my wild grief at the loss of my wife and my pent-up rage at life and death. But also it was an outpouring of joy in my love for her and her love for me, and sudden overwhelming sense of our undying oneness.

Emotions that run too deep may never reach the surface. Now these Christmas gifts from my wife had opened all the secret gates and sluices of my inmost being.

I was drained, but I was filled with an extraordinary sense of release. I was free.

The storm had passed.

I rose from the floor, I took a

My Beloved,

Steady, Jim, steady, dear heart. When you read this, you have survived til Christmas, and the worst is over now. You and I have dreamed dreams and thought thoughts and been, oh, so close, my dearest. If your heart cannot find the answer to "why, why, why," then for the time being please accept my sure faith and firm trust that all is well with me. For you these may yet be aching hours, and I have felt for you and been greatly concerned, but I have been comforted in this thought: Surely in surrendering you to the law of Love, I have also surrendered you to greater growth, greater understanding, and yes, I am sure, to happiness and joy and fulfillment.

bath, I dressed in my best suit and happiest tie, I went out to breakfast and to meet the day.

I ate dinner that day with Mark. After dinner he beat me twice at chess, which made his Christmas a happy one—happier, at least than it might have been—and that made *my* Christmas happier too.

It was late when I got home, late enough for bed. I had left the gifts under the tree. Now I picked them up and looked at them again—the golf balls, "In Memoriam," *Joseph and His Brothers*. I noticed that *Joseph and His Brothers* had 1207 pages; I would not read it tonight. But I scanned the last page, where Joseph tells

his brothers that they are all in a play, God's play, and that it is time to forget about all the ills which occurred—God had turned it to good. I read his concluding words: "It is the future we are interested in. Sleep in peace. Tomorrow in God's good providence we shall take our way back into that quaint and comic land of Egypt."

That seemed a right thought to end the day with, and I was *ready* to end it. I was tired; I had never felt *more* tired. I hardly lay down in bed before I was asleep.

The next morning was a workday again. I arose at the usual time, in the usual way, and went to work.

These Poems Are the Tears
I Kept

If I am being weak when I feel sad
remembering my wife and how she died
and how she lived and all the joy we had
since the loved night when I lay down beside
her for the first time, and she was my wife
and I her husband, and we were in love
with one another and in love with life;
if to be strong is never to think of
the love I had but cannot have again,
or when I think of it to feel no pain
if tears are weakness and not meant for men—
then I am weak, for often I have lain
awake and thought about my wife and wept
for her. These poems are the tears I kept.

Anything Less Than Utter Trust

Anything less than utter trust in life
and love would be like treason to my wife.
Because of what she was, even the pain
was not all loss, something in it was gain;
I come forth stronger than I was, not sad
but with a faith I never knew I had,
the faith that life is good, the strength to press
after a meaning in the meaningless,
the wisdom to submerge the fraction of
myself in the vast integer of love.

Life is a strong urge. It cannot stand still
but must go forward, and there is a will
to live in me, a love of life. To me
if there were nothing in eternity
save life's brief bubble, no immortal soul,
no hope beyond the grave, no God, no goal,
and we were but the children of mischance,
the universe would have significance
because we are and draw this life-stuff, breath!
One moment's life outweighs the whole of death.

I have no reach of thought to comprehend
the meaning of our life or see the end
we serve, but know our limits are not birth
and death, the three dimensions of this Earth.
I have a sense but dimly understood
but still a sense of being used for good;
life's meaning is as far beyond all seeming

grief

as we must be beyond our own cells' dreaming
and what power can they have to understand
what a speech is or the motion of a hand?

Yet more is to be found in us to meet
whatever comes, though it may be defeat;
though we may fall, we do not fall alone,
but share a meaning larger than our own;
we are one with the all; our small selves merge
into the living will, the upward urge
that rises from unfathomable springs
of being, the compassion for all things
that live and feel and suffer; we are part
of one vast action, pulses in one heart.

How shall we count the battle won or lost
or meter out the gain or weigh the cost?
Life has a meaning measured not by length
or even by our weakness or our strength;
not only by bright triumphs and full years
may life be measured, but sometimes by tears.
It is the living, life is measured by;
the aim of life is living. She and I
shared thought and love and passion, watched the light
together and together faced the night.

I was her husband and she was my wife;
life gave itself to us who gave ourselves to life.

Love's Rose

Love has less substance than a lover's breath
heaved in a sigh and spun into a song,
and yet it has a power to outlast death;
Heaven and Earth will not endure as long.
After the fiery twilight of the gods,
when all our demons and our deities
perish together and cast down their rods
and crowns, love will rise weeping from its knees
and raise a world beyond the reach of doom,
that will survive even our unbelief,
that will not wither with the withering bloom
of time or fade with life's fast-fading leaf,
but like a delicate and deathless rose
will blossom and burn red in winter snows.

119

Another Dawn

Faced with the passing of someone we love, our heart cries out in the passion of its loneliness and is not comforted with easy answers.

Our heart tells us that we are meant to live, not to die. We are meant to express life ever more consummately. When someone fails to do this, we wonder why.

To understand the meaning of death, we must understand the meaning of life. Looking at life, we see that all things change. But although all things change, nothing perishes. Things only change.

If this is true in the world of things, how much more true it is in the world of mind! Soul has a substance of its own, no less permanent for being immaterial, no less real for being invisible. We cannot measure it with calipers or weigh it in a balance. We cannot feel it with our fingers or see it with our eyes. But it is there, substantial, real. It changes, but it will not perish.

Life does not begin with birth. It does not end with death. Life is an eternal process, an eternal progress. This visible form, this audible voice, this aggregation of organs, this network of ideas—we are more than these. These are the trappings of visibility. We are an expression of the Spirit of life.

Stand on the shore at night. You can hear the sound of the waves. You can see them break and whiten on the rocks. But the sea itself, vast and imponderable and strange and deep, you cannot see.

The wave breaks on the rocks and then is gone, and all that is left behind is a fading line of foam. Yet the sea is more than the foam that fades on the rock. The sea is more than the wave into which it shaped itself for a moment. When wave and foam are gone, the sea abides to shape itself into another wave and fling itself in foam on the rocks again.

You are like a sea that shapes itself into a wave. The wave will expend itself, but you will not expend yourself. You will shape yourself into an infinity of waves. You are the ever-renewing, ever-unfolding expression of infinite life. You are the spirit of the Infinite moving across infinity.

Eternity is not an alternation of life and nonlife. There is only life. The truth is that we cannot die. For we are life. Life is energy. Life is expression. It cannot cease because it is ceaselessness. We may change form and vanish from view, but we cannot cease to be. We never cease to be, not for a moment. We cannot be separated from life. We cannot be less than life.

Life is a road that winds among the hills of time. With every turn in the road an old view vanishes, a new view appears. Life is a pilgrimage, a passage through eternity, a journey into the unknown. People are as travelers on a journey.

Some pass quickly beyond the bend in the road that hides them from our view. Some walk beside us all the way. Some seem to creep along, and some pass swiftly as a runner. But life cannot be measured in terms of time, only in terms of living.

When people die they do not cease to be; they only pass beyond human sight.

There is a unity beyond the unities of time and place and even thought, a unity that links us as one, just as all the waves are one sea and all the islands one earth. Does not love link us with our friends though they be on the

The wave breaks on the rocks and then is gone, and all that is left behind is a fading line of foam. Yet the sea is more than the foam that fades on the rock. The sea is more than the wave into which it shaped itself for a moment. When wave and foam are gone, the sea abides to shape itself into another wave and fling itself in foam on the rocks again.

You are like a sea that shapes itself into a wave.

grief

other side of the Earth? So those we love may pass beyond the reach of hands but not outside the heart.

Why are we afraid of death? It is because we are afraid of the unknown. Yet is not each new day an adventure into the unknown?

Exactly what is on the other side of death we do not know. But we may be sure that it is life. Life is on the other side of death as it is on this side.

Death is not evil. Neither is it good. Is the turning of a page good or evil? Is the rest between two notes of music good or evil? Is the opening of a door good or evil? Death is an incident. It is a part of life, as sleep is a part of life, as nightfall is a part of life. Sleep gives way to waking. Night turns into day. So death is but the passage from life to life.

Death is a door through which we pass into another room. It is a rest between two notes in an unfinished symphony. It is a page we turn to a new chapter in the book of life. It is not the end; it is a new beginning. It is not the fall of night; it is another dawn.

We may not know just what will occur when we pass through the door. Yet we can trust the Keeper of Infinity. Life is the work of a grand and kind intelligence and has an order and a meaning beyond our power to see. Who among us could have planned an atom or a star? Who could have contrived the Earth, the seasons, the delicate balance of forces that permits life on Earth to exist? What scientist could have fashioned the human body? What philosopher could have thought of the laws that govern mind and space? What poet could have imagined love and wonder?

We can trust this intelligence that made the world. We were not made for dying, or for failure, or for pain. We are meant to live gloriously. We are the children of the Infinite. We have a divine destiny. We are advancing toward this destiny.

Out of the Infinite we came and into the Infinite we return. But we are upward bound. We have risen through an eternity of experiences. We shall go higher yet.

Snow-Flowers

Now winter's flowers fill the air.
How different from the summer kind
they are, but when the fields lie bare,
they look as lovely to my mind.

Where are the daisies half so white
as these brief blossoms of the storm?
As fragile, fair, and pure as light,
almost too beautiful for form.

Summer has flowers, but has none such
as these flung from the wind-tossed bough
of winter, bitter cold to touch!
And still they warm the heart somehow.

The Journey of Today

Dawn is the threshold of today.
Dawn is an open door
that sends you up a sunlit way
you have not climbed before.
But you can know God does not give
you hills too hard to climb;
His love ordains that you shall live
but one day at a time.
Let go dead yesterday's regret,
tomorrow's phantom fear;
live in the living now and let
the present good appear.
Even a stay-at-home must make
the journey of today;
go with a willing heart and take
love's lamp to light your way;
prayer be the staff you lean upon;
with faith your feet be shod.
Today you do not walk alone—
today you walk with God.

Sunrise

Sunrise is never sudden but comes slowly.
Out of His heaven-bowl God pours His holy
water of clear and crystal light to run
through the rose window of His perfect sun
and fall into our mind. In the beginning
we sense not light so much as darkness thinning;
dawn touches first the tips and tops of things—
the mind to catch the morning must have wings,
and when the day is cloudy, day may start
not so much in the sky as in our heart.
Yet after a while, all imperceptibly,
we rise and look around us—and we see!

VIII.

Faith

Transformation

In the invisible God's tireless hand
fashions the wonder that at last appears,
transmuting the dull stuff of circumstance
into the rainbow shimmer of romance;
and he that can sees pearls in grains of sand,
diamonds in coal, fresh poems in stale tears.

The ugly duckling, hoping it would die,
had never dreamed it might become a swan;
the worm all humbly goes and never knows
that one day it will be a butterfly;
the night does not anticipate the dawn;
the thorn has no foreknowledge of the rose.

Who has the faith and foresight to surmise
what mighty unseen changes life has wrought?
Out of the chrysalis of our defeat
bursts greater glory than we ever thought,
and he who does not blindly shut his eyes
may find a rainbow in a muddy street!

127

The Original Look

It is as if we are on a sea voyage. We see far away what looks to be a mist take shape out of the waves. Then we see that what we took to be a mist now seems to be a mountain. As we approach yet closer we see that it is not a mountain but an island. And on still closer view, the island is seen to have many mountains, valleys, beaches, harbors, houses, wharves, roads, people, animals, trees, fields, and gardens.

And if we look at a blade of grass growing in one of these gardens—look clearly enough, keenly enough—will we not see that the grass is no more what our first careless glance considers it than the island is the mist we first took it to be?

This that seems a blade of grass will reveal itself to be an island, with its own multitudinous features as distinct and various as mountains, beaches, living creatures, fields and gardens, blades of grass. And beyond this, are there not yet further islands? Islands hardly dreamed-of, undiscovered, unexplored, unknown!

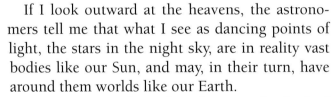

If I look outward at the heavens, the astronomers tell me that what I see as dancing points of light, the stars in the night sky, are in reality vast bodies like our Sun, and may, in their turn, have around them worlds like our Earth.

One time I saw through a telescope what looked like a little patch of light.

"That is the nebula in Andromeda," said the astronomer. "This little patch of light that in the telescope looks like a puff of cotton or a bit of milkweed down, too faint to find when you take your eye from the eyepiece, is an island universe containing millions of stars, millions of suns like our own. The whole night sky sprinkled with all the stars that sparkle overhead is not so large as this puff of cotton. And this—which is almost a million light-years away—is but the nearest of myriads of such universes that astronomers have located in space."

What a world God has made!

My sense and senses shout it, and the physicists corroborate it.

Sometimes I think that physicists have more imagination than poets.

Physicists describe the world as a dance of electric particles.

The world dances!

As it dances, it sings. Had we the instruments, we could hear the harmonies.

Our world is made of light, living, singing light, dancing on its everlasting journey round the throne of the Eternal, who sent it winging on His word!

God said, "Let there be light." Having made light, what a stuff God had to make the world of.

God took the light—and was the light the movement of God's thought upon the deep?—and some of the light God made whirl in the patterns of the dance that we call matter—but it is still more light than matter. What are heaven and Earth but the momentary shape of motion?

What a world God has made!
My sense and senses shout it, and the physicists corroborate it.
Sometimes I think that physicists have more imagination than poets.
Physicists describe the world as a dance of electric particles.

The world dances!

As it dances, it sings. Had we the instruments, we could hear the harmonies.

faith

Oh, the rainbow world we live in! Rivers of light pour everywhere, too luminous to see, showers and cascades of light. Children of light, we are ourselves the light. Swimmers in electric seas, we are ourselves the electric stuff.

This is the way God made the world.

This is the way we should see it.

It is all good. It is all beautiful. It is all extraordinary.

Nothing is plain or stale.

Nothing is inconsequential.

Nothing is to be overlooked.

How much better to mistake ordinary things to be divine than to take divine things to be ordinary!

How much better like an ancient savage to feel that a stone may be God than like a modern savant to feel that God may be no more than a stone!

Out of a clod of clay God made the first human.

All the fantastic world of living forms we see around us—what is this but clay that would not lie still? And what clay ever lies still? Behind the inert seeming, streams of electrons leap and circle in a flaming dance.

It is not enough to see God in extraordinary things. It is necessary to see that ordinary things are extraordinary too.

God does not create two things

alike. Not two human beings. Not two cherry trees. Not two blades of grass.

When we are skillful enough to measure them, we will find that God never makes two electrons alike.

God is the infinite creativity fashioning out of His infinite thought the infinite world of force and form.

I wake in the morning and I accept this morning just as if it were like the mornings when I waked before.

How can I be so dull of perception?

This morning—like every morning—is an original creation.

Last night a freezing mist fell. This morning the world is the jewel box of God. Every tree, every bush is diamonded. Every frozen twig glitters till I hardly know whether this is ice or fire. Every tremor of the wind strikes from the crystal world blue-white and golden flames.

Today it would be hard to miss the glory. But how often we shut our eyes and complain because there is nothing to see.

We shut our ears and wonder why we never hear anything and why nobody ever has anything to say.

We never get quiet and look

130

for God or listen for God's voice, so we say that God does not exist, or if He does, God is distant and indifferent.

How long has it been since you saw the dawn? A few mornings ago I arose before the sun and saw the light come spreading across the fields. Little pink clouds formed in the sky, looking as if they might be the sun's breath misting.

How long has it been since you blew your breath on an icy morning and watched it mist?

How long has it been since you noticed how things look when there is fog? Trees and towers evaporate halfway up. You have a sense of the intangibility of things. Things are but dream-shapes drifting in your mind and any moment may dissolve. The world is something you have only half imagined. You are detached and alone on an island of thought.

How long has it been since you walked in the half-world of moon-light, upon the bottom of the sea of night, where all things look as if they were awash in pearly tides?

How long has it been since you looked at snow, examined its star-shapes under a magnifying glass, or held out your tongue and let snowflakes melt on it as they fell?

How long has it been since you looked at frost-ferns growing on a windowpane? More mutable than grass, more delicate than flowers, blow lightly on them for a moment and they vanish.

How long has it been since you watched the city lights come on in the evening? the street lights blossoming along the avenues like golden flowers and the little lights in people's houses, warm, glowing squares of life?

How long has it been since you watched the people pouring out of offices and factories and felt the pulsing, surging, jostling tide of city life?

How long has it been since you

Last night a freezing mist fell. This morning the world is the jewel box of God. Every tree, every bush is diamonded. Every frozen twig glitters till I hardly know whether this is ice or fire. Every tremor of the wind strikes from the crystal world blue-white and golden flames.
Today it would be hard to miss the glory. But how often we shut our eyes and complain because there is nothing to see.

sat still and looked at things by candlelight?

How long has it been since you listened to birds sing or watched them fly? I throw a few crumbs under the small tree outside my kitchen window, and to it by the dozens sparrows fly, hovering, pirouetting, twittering. Sparrows are grace in flight. Sometimes such swarms of them alight in the bare branches that I have a tree of birds. How long has it been since you looked at the bare branches of a tree? If the moon is full tonight, go out and watch it rise through the branches of a tree. The moon of winter, like a golden bird caught in a black net, will slip upward through the lacy interstices and at last soar free.

If we do not look at things, we cannot complain that life has nothing to look at. It is our look, not our lives, that becomes humdrum.

Not long ago a friend and I went for a winter hike at Unity Village. A narrow creek wanders through the back hills. The weather having been dry and cold, the water was dried up or frozen, so we could walk down in the creek bed. The banks rose high and steep above

> If we do not look at things, we cannot complain that life has nothing to look at. It is our look, not our lives, that becomes humdrum.

our heads, and in the meanders of this ravine we were soon altogether separated from the fields and woods above. Never farther than a few miles from home, I could not have been farther from everything familiar if I had gone ten thousand miles. The world was my usual world, but I was having an original look at it.

We walk into a familiar room and see nothing in it. We know it so well that we can find our way around in it with our eyes shut. And this is what we do.

After a while the world becomes such a room.

Have you let time's dust settle on the window? When a child finds dust on a windowpane, he writes his name in it or draws a picture. Dust, too, can disclose a world.

Things are wonderful beyond our farthest imagining. For things are God's imagining. But you are God's imagining too. God made you in His image.

And God gave you an original look. This is the look that a child has. This is the look that God has. This is the look with which God looked at everything He had made and saw that it was good.

The Pollyanna

There are four possible attitudes to take in a situation.

You can believe that things are going to work out and work hard to see that they do.

You can believe that things are going to work out and do nothing about them yourself.

You can believe that things are not going to work out but nevertheless work hard yourself.

You can believe that things are not going to work out and resign yourself to defeat.

It is easy to see that the second and fourth attitudes have little to recommend them.

The one who has the third attitude may succeed in his endeavors, but how he suffers with them. "This is a hard, hard task," he groans under the heavy burden not only of his task but of his thoughts about it.

Surely the first attitude is best of all. The person who has it is most likely to succeed, and what is more, she has a spirit of joy as she works toward success.

Those who think of themselves as deep enough to be discouraged about things say that those who are encouraged about things have a shallow view of life; they call such people *Pollyannas*.

If a Pollyanna is someone who refuses to face facts, certainly none of us wants to be one. We cannot get rid of facts by pretending that they are not there. But we can face facts and still know that good is there, whether we can see it at first or not. It has to be there because God is there. And we can seek in every situation to find and bring forth God's good.

A Pollyanna is not a person who refuses to face facts. He is a person who refuses to accept them. He does not believe that the passing facts are the ultimate truth. The ultimate truth is always good. This is a good world. It is good because God who made it is good. Because God who made it is good, there must be good in everything. The Pollyanna, the positive thinker, the Unity student looks for this good and does all he can to bring it forth.

Jesus refused to be limited by

faith

facts. No matter what appearances might be, he looked for the good, expected the good, and did all he could to bring forth the good. Jesus knew that the world is the work of the good God. He was in the Good Presence always. Good was never far from him.

When he was asked to feed the multitude that had come to hear him and found out that they had only a few loaves and fishes, he did not say that the facts indicated he would not be able to do it. Beyond the facts he saw the everywhere-at-hand bounty of God, and he called it forth and fed the people.

Even when they told him that Lazarus was three days dead, he did not submit to the fact of death. Instead he decreed, expecting the good, "Lazarus, come forth" (Jn. 11:43 KJV).

Remember how much Jesus approved of the army captain who asked Jesus to heal his servant. When Jesus offered to go, the captain told him it would not be necessary. "Only speak the word, and my servant will be healed" (Mt. 8: 8), the army captain said. Why did Jesus think so highly of this man? Because here was a man of faith like himself; here was a man who expected and believed in the possibility of good.

Jesus did not see a hungry multitude; he saw them fed by the infinite bounty. He did not see sick people; he saw them whole, alive with the aliveness of divine life. He did not see drab facts; he saw the radiant truth. "You will know the truth, and the truth will make you free" (Jn. 8:32) Jesus said. "Be of good cheer" (Jn. 16: 33 KJV).

Never once did Jesus say to anyone who came to him for help, "You have to accept the facts." He said over and over in many different words, Ask and it shall be given unto you; seek, and ye shall find; knock, and it shall be opened unto you.

I like the story of the little girl who looked up at the church steeple and said, "What's the plus sign doing up there?" It is more than a coincidence that the symbol of Christianity, the cross, is also a plus sign, the sign of the positive, the positive-minded, the positive-hearted.

Usually when people start talking about facing facts, they mean looking at the worst side of them. Facts are many-sided. Is it wrong to look for the best side rather than the worst?

It is said that Thomas Edison made 10,000 experiments that failed before he made an electric

134

If a Pollyanna is someone who refuses to face facts, certainly none of us wants to be one. We cannot get rid of facts by pretending that they are not there. But we can face facts and still know that good is there, whether we can see it at first or not. It has to be there because God is there. And we can seek in every situation to find and **bring forth God's good.**

bulb that lighted. What a fantastic amount of foolish optimism he must have had! Could someone who thought things were going to turn out badly have kept going? I do not believe it.

Wilhelm Roentgen came to work one morning and found that a photographic plate he had left in a drawer was fogged. He might have bemoaned the fact. Instead, he discovered X rays—and opened the atomic age.

An apple fell and hit Sir Isaac Newton on the head. The fact is that the apple probably raised a lump—but the truth is that it brought forth the theory of gravitation.

In the Nova Scotia mine explosion of 1958, men were entombed

for days without light, food, or water. They were keenly aware of their plight, but when one of them became depressed, the others crept around him and said all the things they could think of to encourage him. They would not let themselves stop believing in rescue. They would not let themselves stop expecting rescue.

After days of almost unbelievable endurance, rescue came. It is hard to believe that the attitude of the men did not make a difference in their survival. But the point I am trying to make is that their attitude is the one to take, whatever the outcome. It is better to go down to defeat believing in victory, affirming it and striving for it to the end and helping others to strive for it to the end, than to go down believing in defeat, expecting and submitting to it.

Faith leads human beings to try all sorts of things, some that they fail at. We can be grateful for this—for many of those who failed at first have gone on to win ultimate victory or prepare the way for others to win it. And only those who have dared to go beyond their depth have added to the stature of the human race.

Charles Fillmore believed that he would live forever. Do you think he would have lived a more useful life if at ten he had accepted the fact that he was a hopeless invalid? He lived to be ninety-three. He cofounded Unity and ran it. He wrote, lectured, traveled, lived actively when he was in his nineties. He influenced millions of persons.

I like the story of the little girl who looked up at the church steeple and said, "What's the plus sign doing up there?" It is more than a coincidence that the symbol of Christianity, the cross, is also a plus sign, the sign of the positive, the positive-minded, the positive-hearted.

And he taught them to believe in the good. He taught them to keep believing. He taught them to keep acting on their belief.

I wonder how many of us can continue to apply ourselves with spirit to a task once we have become convinced that we cannot succeed at it. Even the heroine who stands by her post and refuses to flee although she knows she will be overwhelmed makes her stand precisely because she believes that good will come out of what she is doing. She is able to make her stand because she knows, perhaps not consciously but in the deep core of her being, that she is "a part of all that's good, and good shall be victorious."

This is a knowledge that all of us have access to, and I think we know it most clearly in moments of crisis. Then our eyes are lifted to it, and we catch a glimpse of the eternal Truth shining through the changing facts.

On one of the dark nights of my own spirit, I wrote this poem. I think it contains a truth:

How much the human spirit
outweighs the human pain—
so much that no experience
but can be counted gain!

What faith before impossibles
a man is capable of
who, being overwhelmed,
yet trusts that God is love!

What doubter dares to say
man is not god or near it
when even his defeats become
the triumph of his spirit!

A pessimist may ask, "How can you look at things and take a positive attitude?" But I ask, "How can you look at things and take any other?"

"If we had never before looked upon the earth," wrote Richard Jefferies, "but suddenly came to it man or woman grown, set down in the midst of a summer mead, would it not seem to us a radiant vision?"

Copernicus, looking at the heavens, exclaimed, "All I can do is adore!"

Someone asked William Blake, "When the sun rises do you not see a round disc of fire, somewhat like a guinea?" "Oh, no," said Blake, "I see an innumerable company of the heavenly host crying, 'Holy, holy, holy is the Lord God, the Almighty.'"

Oh, the unbelievable, unexplainable, fantastic, marvelous world! Too vast, too varied to be comprehended with all our sense and senses! And most marvelous of all the marvels, the human being!

One of the oldest and most universal of stories is the story of the baby born to a king who in one way or another is taken from the palace and brought up as a woodchopper or a swineherd or in some other lowly position. Then, when he is grown, he makes his way back to the palace, and there finds out that he is not a woodchopper but a king's son. And immediately that is what he is. Because the truth is, that is what he always was. He is a king's son; he merely believed he was a woodchopper; and he has only to see the truth to come into his birthright.

faith

This is what the positive thinkers believe about all of us. We look at human beings and see the woodchopper, but we also see the king's son. We look at the world and see the facts and flaws, but we also see the divine perfection working to come forth.

Down through the centuries there have been many to say, "It won't work." "Nothing good can come out of this." "It's hopeless." Even, "The world is coming to an end."

Yet after thousands of years of chance and change, we are still pursuing the great and unpredictable adventure that is life; there are more of us than there have ever been; we are healthier, more intelligent, more understanding, more generous, more human-hearted.

I wonder how much the human race has ever been helped by those who pointed out the dreadful state of affairs. Suppose they were right. Whom would you want at your side in the mine disaster? One of them, prophesying destruction? Or someone with courage, faith, and hope, someone with a cheerful word and a friendly hand on your shoulder in the dark, trying to find a way out and helping you to find your way out too?

A friend of mine won a citation in World War I because when the engineers he was with were pinned down on a hillside by enemy fire, he kept them singing while they worked.

Singing under fire! Whispering to a downcast friend in a mine disaster all the reasons you can think of why he will be rescued! Pollyanna foolishness! Surely, but it is out of such brave and wonderful human foolishness that human progress and endurance have come.

Thank God for the ones with a word of cheer, a smile of encouragement, a thought of hope! Thank God that in times of trouble most of us become Pollyannas, believing in the good, seeking the good, and helping others to believe in it and seek it. If this were not so, the human race would have vanished long ago—obliterated not by events but by its own discouragement.

As I have written somewhere—at least, I should have written it—I may not know who will win the race, but I do know who will lose it—it will be the one who loses faith and gives up.

Never lose faith. Never give up.

If in the end the world comes tumbling down, I hope I shall hear, across the tumult of the falling stars, some Roland of that un-imagined age blowing his death-less horn at Roncesvalles, blowing his defiance of all that is less than might have been, blowing his faith

that the good will triumph yet.

And if I am there, I pray that I will put my horn to my lips, too, and blow my note of courage for my friends to hear and take heart by.

Thank God for the ones with a word of cheer, a smile of encouragement, a thought of hope! Thank God that in times of trouble most of us become Pollyan-nas, **believing in the good,** seeking the good, and help-ing others to believe in it and seek it. If this were not so, the hu-man race would have vanished long ago— obliterated not by events but by its own discouragement.

March Weed

March green brings spring's first beauty—it is shy—
some looking here see weeds and turn away.
But I see life, crack-crowding, winter-braving,
with all its wonder, all its flame flags waving,
hear here its gay triumphing trumpets play!

There's something about green things that starts hearts singing,
pushing up at the sky,
pushing through death's debris
airily, merrily, verily
life out of death springing!

This is the valor passing duty—
May's pink-white perfect loveliness
has not this beauty,
this touch to heal and bless:

Flowers are but weeds that know their places,
flowers are weeds with happy faces.

Oh, Yes, for You!

Now small leaves open, small birds sing,
small streams run full, and it is spring;
the winter melts to its icy core.
Hey, you there, what are you waiting for?
Have you woes so deep and hopes so few
that spring can come back and not for you?

If leaf and stream and bird can tell
when it is spring, you know as well;
you have a green life as much as a tree,
and like a spring freshet your thought can run free,
and more than a bird, if you've faith to try,
you can rise in your spirit and sing and fly!

Invisibles

O the invisible air
I scarcely know is there!
I cannot feel its press,
it seems but emptiness,
but empty seeming,
yet it is teeming.

Reality may be
something we cannot see,
yet no less real for being
too clear for seeing.

"Help Thou Mine Unbelief"

Faith is not so much a matter of the mind as of the heart. Sometimes in seeking to understand God as a principle, we lose sight of God as a presence. Theologians and philosophers can know God as words to set down in books, but a child that cannot even utter the name of God may have a faith beyond that of learned priests. To have faith is not to theorize about God or even to imagine God, but to **experience God.**

"Lord, I believe; help thou mine unbelief." Out of how many troubled hearts this cry has risen!

For some it is easy to believe. To them God is as real as their own hands or eyes; God's purposes are plain, God's love is sure. They may not be able to put their faith into words. They do not need to. They have it in their hearts, and they put it into all they say and do.

For others it is not easy to believe. They want to believe. They pore over books of metaphysics and study the teachings of mystics and saints. They spend long hours in prayer. Yet they lack a heart of faith. Even after years the mists of doubt remain, the weary cry still rises: "Help thou mine unbelief."

143

Virginia Love and Jim Freeman.

faith

Faith is the foundation of religion. Psychologists analyze its nature. Mystics describe its effects. Theologians dispute its meaning. When we hear of miracles, we hear that they were wrought through faith. When we pray and do not get what we pray for, we are likely to be told that we do not have enough faith.

What is this faith that we are told is so important to us?

Faith is not so much a matter of the mind as of the heart. Sometimes in seeking to understand God as a principle, we lose sight of God as a presence. Theologians and philosophers can know God as words to set down in books, but a child that cannot even utter the name of God may have a faith beyond that of learned priests. To have faith is not to theorize about God or even to imagine God, but to experience God.

Faith is the opposite of fear. Have you ever felt the icy feet, the racing heart, the unnerved hands of fear? The hands of faith are strong and sure. The feet of faith move steady to the will. The heart of faith beats quietly in tune with God. Faith is a warmth, a feeling of well-being that envelops the body and overflows the mind. Faith brings an inward peace, a tranquil spirit.

Faith is the expectation of the unexpected. Faith is an open and courageous heart. The arms of faith are outstretched, not in supplication but in surrender to life's sovereign will, in submission to the ruling order of the universe, in receptivity to good.

Faith is the power to see in the disappointment of today the fulfillment of tomorrow, in the end of old hopes the beginning of new life. Faith is the inward power to see beyond the outward signs, the power to know that all is right when everything looks wrong.

When our fondest dreams seem to go amiss and our dearest prayers seem to remain unanswered, faith is a vision of life that soars beyond the limitations of the self—these narrow senses, this imperfect reason, this drift of circumstance—and sees that our life is a part of something more than we have ever understood. In spite of all that may seem and all that may happen there is an ultimate fulfillment, that all is truly well, that all must be well. Life has an eternal meaning, we are one with the infinite, and whatever may befall us, in the all-infolding, all-unfolding everness of God, life will work out for good.

To have such faith is to have the serenity of the saint, the passion of the poet, and the exaltation of the mystic.

You can learn to have faith.

Faith is not an abstraction; it is an attitude toward life, a feeling about life. It does not come out of signs or miracles or any outward happenings so much as out of inward growth.

If you cannot believe in much, then believe in the little that you can. Start where you are and grow. What seed can have a foreknowledge of the tree it will become? What thorny bush can prophesy the rose? What worm can tell of the butterfly? Faith grows.

If you find yourself deploring how little your faith is, think how far you have come with the little faith you have. As you climb a hill it is sometimes well to look back to see how far you have come instead of always looking at the interminable heights ahead.

Sometimes you may have more faith than you imagine, and when you need it, you will find it there within you.

Have you never, standing by the sea or walking down a country road or wandering through a field or wood or gazing at the starry sky, suddenly been lifted up and out of yourself, overwhelmed by beauty, so that for a moment you were not anything at all, but were a part of all that is? Surely this is faith.

Have you never stood on a busy corner and felt your heart go out, clear out, to the people, all the people, your people, feeling their minds all winged with dreams like yours, feeling their hearts all big with yearnings like yours, feeling the human tide of life moving, ceaselessly moving, moving forward? Surely this is faith.

Have you never in the silence of yourself felt a sense of being more than self? Surely this is faith.

Faith grows.

And the faith that grows out of questioning is stronger than the faith born of blind acceptance. It can withstand the shocks of circumstance. Only one who questions the universe and questions it in utter honesty can grow in his or her comprehension of the truth.

Sometimes when we have much to meet, we doubt our power to meet it. We feel alone. Yet if we but keep on, we will not fail, we cannot fail—even if we falter, even if we fall. Even in defeat we are victorious; for we win the greatest victory of all, victory over ourselves.

This is certain; we are not

If you cannot believe in much, then
believe in the little that you can.
Start where you are and grow.
What seed can have a foreknowledge
of the tree it will become? What
thorny bush can prophesy the rose?
What worm can tell of the butterfly?

Faith grows.

alone. We are one with the sovereign and sustaining will, one with the abiding order, one with the goodness and the heroism, one with the upward urge, one with the triumphant spirit of life.

Though there be no shouts of praise, no laurels, we bear the whole race forward in our great stride, and the compassion that infolds the world catches us to ourselves and presses us even into the inmost heart of life, even into the love of God Himself.

"Lord, I believe; help thou mine unbelief."

When from your heart the troubled cry goes up, know that there is no cry but that somehow there is an answer. There is a love. There is a power. There is a wisdom, and there is a way to go. Let your heart hold fast; the way will be made plain.

faith

Mountains Affirm

Mountains have sun-crowned slopes and wear snow's white;
there is a grandeur in their untrod height;
they stand as firm as faith, yet soar like prayer.
Mountains are affirmations. They declare
the absolute and have a power to bless
my spirit with infolding quietness.
Mountains remind me that I have in me
an untouched summit of serenity,
abiding, crowned with majesty, untrod,
upsoaring. Mountains make me think of God.

As Still as Snow

It is not hard to be aware
when all goes well that God is there;
but in my winter moments, when
doubts buffet my bare spirit, then
it is that I must find God real.

And it is then I pray and feel
God's peace upon my mind come down
like nightfall on a noisy town,
God's love upon my heart as still
as snow upon a winter hill.

faith

Crocus

I wonder if a crocus
wishes to come out;
I think it must, like you and me,
have many times of doubt.

And draw inside its dreary bulb
and peering at the snow
that fills the wide and wintry world
mistrust its power to grow.

Yet once it takes its heart in hand
and steps into the cold,
it finds itself clothed like a king
in purple robes and gold.

Grace

Though God, God only, can create,
I till and weed, and then I wait,
and in the thicket of my thought
bloom flowers that I never wrought.
I stand in wonder and behold
beauty I never sowed unfold,
visions of faith, insights of love,
truths that I had no forethought of.

Somehow there is in me yet more
than I myself might settle for,
a faith that brings perfection out
past my own powers. I have no doubt
one day all unexpectedly
the rose of Christ shall bloom in me.

IX.

Prayer

Homeward

Home the shepherd and the sheep
come at evening from the hill,
through a silence kind and deep,
full of shadows soft and still.
Still and soft and deep and kind
the gentle blessing of a prayer
falls like evening on the mind.
Homeward from the hills of care
now my thoughts return like sheep.
I shall pray and pray until
peace comes dropping down like sleep,
and I am home, and I am still.

A Wind and a Tide

Do not settle for little dreams.
You are yourself the dream of God who dreamed the Sun and stars.
And He meant you for more.

That is why you hear forever the cry for more in your flesh.

That is why you cannot be content with littleness; you can accept it, but you cannot be content.

The flowers in your garden open and close.

The birds fly south in autumn and north again in spring.

The Earth spins shining around the Sun, singing psalms of day and night.

The Sun and all the stars breathe in and out and ebb and flow to winds and tides of a sea too vast for our imagining.

Listen.

Be still.

Then, perhaps, if you are still enough, you can hear the everlasting tide of being flinging itself on the shore of forever. The tides that run in all Earth's oceans are mere ripples in a pond compared to this tide.

And it pulses for you.

Perhaps, if you are still enough, you can hear the universe breathing in and breathing out again. All the winds that sweep Earth's ocean of air—zephyrs and breezes and gales and hurricanes—are like a child's blowing of bubbles compared to this breath.

And it breathes for you.

There is a wind that blows over the world.

There is a tide that moves the world of space and all the worlds beyond the world of space.

This wind, I think, is the breath of God, and this tide is the pulsing of God's heart.

The Way of Attunement

There is a way to get the power of God to do what we want it to do; to heal us when we need healing; to supply our needs when we feel lack; to comfort us when we are troubled; to bring us friends when we are lonely, joy for grief, and peace for pain; to light our path when we are lost and wander frightened in the dark.

It is the way that a rainbow is made after rain. It is the way that morning is made to follow night and spring is made to come after winter.

It is the way that a bare branch brings forth green leaves.

It is the way that the mist rises out of the sea, and the way that an ugly waterbug changes into a dragonfly.

Do you know this way?

It is the way of attunement.

It is the way of being one with the way of things.

At the core of being is a rhythm; when you place yourself in tune with this cosmic rhythm, all things work together for you and you work in harmony with all things.

There is a way of things. That is all you can say of it.

But learn the way of things and follow the way—walk in the way, work in the way—and everything will go your way.

The universe is God's work. He made it very good. He made it to bring forth good. He made it to move and grow, to unfold and expand. When you move with the universe, the universe moves with you—and through you and for you.

Then there is nothing you cannot do or be because all the forces of the universe—all the expanding energies of life—are focused in you and pour through you to come into expression.

The miracle-workers—whether you call them scientists or saints, or children of God—are always the ones who learn the way of things and live in accord with it.

They recognize the power that is there; they study it until they see how it works; then they work with it—and it works through them. They lift their hands; they utter the word—and the power rushes forth!

Then the rest of us stand round and gaze open-mouthed in awe, beholding the healing, or the thunderbolt; the light for our house, or for our mind; the turning wheels, or the overturned world; the life where no life was expected to be!

Set your will against the will of the way of things, and the Supreme Will will hurl you down against yourself, a tiny, shivering, impotent islet of lonely self-ness.

But walk in the way and work with its will, and you will find that the Supreme Will is working only to fulfill the dearest desires of your heart.

Like King Canute, you can wade into the sea and forbid the rising tide to rise. The tide, un-heeding of your paltry crown, will tumble you into the waves.

But make yourself a channel through which the power of the tide may express itself; study how the tide works and do what you have to do to let it work through you—and the tide will do all your work for you.

What gift will it not come bringing you? It will make you not a little King Canute, but serve you as a son of the King of Kings.

When we learn how the tide turns, we learn that it turns for us. Let it turn as it will, and it will take you where you will.

When we learn how the wind blows, we learn that it blows for us. Let it blow as it will, and it will take you where you will.

Not by Might

How few the things that can be done by might!
High aims are thwarted by excess of will;
only when thought is free can mind take flight.
I do not have to press, but to be still.
I fish, but it is God who fills the net;
I dig, but it is God who fills the well;
life is not mine to order but to let
its living power flow through me and impel
me forward. Would I grasp infinity?
I cannot by hard striving reach the goal,
but I can let the Infinite use me
and know my instant oneness with the whole.
I cannot find You, God, by seeking far,
but I am quiet—and there, God, You are!

Revelation

"Give me a revelation, Lord!"
the young man cried in despair.
Spring bloomed, and he rejoiced to see
spring's beauty everywhere,
spring green on every bush, spring birds,
spring flowers in the air.

But, "Give me a revelation, Lord!"
he cried. Love filled his life
and blessed him with good pleasant friends
and a fair, gentle wife
and a gift to lift men's hearts and bring
peace to their inward strife.

But, "Give me a revelation, Lord!"
he cried. He strove to do
as well as he knew how the work
that he was fitted to,
and to what truth he thought he saw
he labored to be true.

But, "Give me a revelation, Lord!"
still constantly he cried.
How often must the Lord have wished
to draw the youth aside
and whisper gently in his ear,
"Dear child, how I have tried!"

Fragile Things

How fragile is a flower!
It may not last an hour;
even more fragile are imaginings.

Yet thoughts and flowers both
possess the gift of growth.
I wonder at the strength of fragile things:

on a harsh peak, where rock
is shattered by the shock
of wind and frost, a fragile flower survives

and one Christ-centered thought,
too tenuous to be caught,
alters the whole direction of our lives.

How Did You Turn It Off?

I said to the Master, "How do I turn on the power of God?"
The Master said, "How did you turn it off?"

Then I saw that if the power of God should be turned off even for a moment, the universe would crash to an end and crumble into nothingness.

The power of God is at work in every atom.

The power of God is at work in every mind.

The power of God is at work in you.

Night and day, pouring forth power, sending power surging through every trembling wire, the dynamos are at work in a city, whether the city wakes or sleeps.

Night and day, the power of God is at work, whether you turn it on or not. Whether you are awake to it or not, whether you know it or not, whether you invite it or not, the power is at work.

And it is at work in you.

You can refuse to use the power consciously—that is all.

But always, when you refuse to use the power consciously, the power may unconsciously use you.

The power of God presses at every point of being, waiting to be drawn forth.

How do you draw it forth?

Is not the best way to let it draw you forth?

For you can use the power of God to the extent of your capacity, but God uses you to the extent of His capacity.

Your wisdom is limited but God's wisdom has no limits.

So when you let God use you as God finds good, who can foresee what good will be brought forth?

The Master Sat Silent

I said to the Master, "Shall I do outer things as well as sit in silent meditation and pray?"

The Master sat silent.

After a time I said again, "Please, Master. Shall I do outer things as well as pray?"

The Master continued to sit silent.

I reached out and caught his sleeve, and I said once more, louder than before, "Master, Master, answer me."

Then he said, "Is not your own insistence that I speak to you your answer? Here I sit in silent meditation. But you would have me do more. You would have me speak to you."

Life is not for praying; prayer is for living. Prayer is part of life—and should be part of life—but life is more than prayer.

Life halloos in your ear and tugs at your sleeve and beckons you to be up and at your tasks.

Go sit in silent meditation on an anthill—and then ask your question.

If a woman comes to us for help, let us help her in every way we can.

If a man comes hungry and I have food, what kind of prayer will I make, feasting at my laden table, staring at his gaunt face? To share my food with him and also to share my heart with him—what prayer is more powerful than this?

How can I feed the man if I do not love him, and how can I love the man if I do not feed him?

For the bread I give him without love will be a beggar's bread and will leave him starving of spirit. And the love I give him without bread will be a miser's love and will leave me starving of spirit.

If we can bind up wounds, dare we leave another bleeding?

If we can speak words of courage, dare we leave another without hope?

If we have a hand to reach and a heart to give, dare we leave another in the pit?

And if we are ourself the one in the pit, then let us reach out our hand to help ourself.

Life has not given us these hands merely to fold in prayer. Life has not given us this heart that it should harden itself against pity.

Life has given us imagination and courage and love and strength to devise and dare and carry out.

Whatever we have to do, let us do everything we can. If we cannot do anything, let us stand and wait!

Standing and waiting can be a kind of doing too.

We can pray when we are standing and waiting. We can pray when we are digging and building and running and lifting too.

Always we should do all we can.

To go beyond our own resources, we have first to come to the end of them.

Sir Alexander Fleming discovered penicillin when a mold got into his test tube. But Sir Alexander Fleming had been seeking healing agents all his life!

Charles Goodyear discovered how to vulcanize rubber when he happened to be cooking a stew pot full of the stuff and some ran over on the kitchen stove. But Charles Goodyear had spent twenty years and all his fortune trying to find how to vulcanize rubber!

When David went out against Goliath, I am sure he prayed—David was a praying man—but also he used what he had to use. This was not much, a sling and a stone, but he used it—and it was enough.

To pray is to ask and affirm.

To pray is also to sow and till.

For to ask and affirm is to sow and till in spirit.

And to sow and till is to ask and affirm of the earth.

When the inward and the outward man are one, then we pray with our whole being. When our whole being moves in one direction, then all the forces of life are drawn together and rush forward to bring the prayer we make to fruition.

A Further Digression on Truths

I hope that you have not been brainwashed by the Western illusion that Truth can only be stated in a scientific formula or as historical fact, and so dismiss stories like the tale of a Virgin Mother as foolish fable.

What a limited view of things to believe that Truth is always facts or that facts are always true!

St. George and his dragon are just as real as an atom.

Genesis is just as true as Darwin's *The Origin of Species*.

And the Easter story has much more truth in it than, for instance, Josephus' "History of the Jews," which makes doubtful mention of it.

Long before we knew anything about scientific formulas or historical facts, humanity was finding truths and trying to express them.

We have painted them and sung them and recited them and acted them out in rites.

We were doing this before we had words to express Truth in.

Without words we were expressing Truth very well.

Words are at most secondhand conveyors of Truth.

They serve best in intellectual matters, which are only a small part of our concern.

Try to tell me what spring is like, for instance.

Spring is certainly a truth—I don't believe anyone would deny this.

To tell me what spring is like, you are going to have to write a lot of books about astronomy and the Earth's orbit around the Sun and the equinox and meteorology and the movement of air masses and biology and migratory birds and recurring vegetation—and I wonder after all your mountain of books if I will have even the foggiest notion what spring is. I don't care how many scientific formulas you give me for chlorophyll and photosynthesis and mitosis—and how many historical facts as to the exact day and hour when the swallows come back to Capistrano.

You would do better to have a poet read me a poem or a painter paint me a picture.

Go out and fetch me a handful of daffodils or violets, or a broken branch of pussy willow or peach blossoms—and I have the truth of spring itself.

Or take me out to frolic with you across the fields and woods of a May morning.

That will be truth enough for me.

Or let us consider a drink of cold water.

There is no question, is there, that water quenches thirst?

This is a truth—and men and women have known it long before we were human. My cat knows it. Any flying bug knows it. Even the willow tree that clogs my sewer knows it.

But I defy you to convey this truth to me by talking to me about the physical and chemical properties of water and the human body. You can talk about specific gravity and H_2O and cell structure and osmosis till your throat is dry—and I will know little more about the power of water to quench thirst than I did when you began.

Pour me a glass of cold water from your pitcher and let me drink—and you need say nothing at all.

Or take love—the love of a young man and a young woman.

I am sure that physiology textbooks and psychology textbooks can give me useful information. But love—physical love—is more than anything a tumult in the blood, a fire in the flesh, a drunkenness of spirit, and conscription of the mind that overpower a whole world of regimented naysaying to plant love's lusty yea in the central citadel of life.

Prayer is related to the class of truths that love and spring and a drink of cold water belong to.

The very word *miracle* has a kind of unscientific, unhistorical air about it.

So does God, when you come to think of it. But the fact that I cannot express God in a mathematical equation or write God's definitive biography does not make God less real. It makes God more real. It makes God more God.

I can know God not by reading a book about God, but by reaching out to God.

Then God becomes as real as spring, as love, as a drink of cold water.

God is a drink of cold water when I am spiritually thirsty—a drink of living water. I can reach out to God in prayer.

And so can you.

Mind's Millpond

How welcome is the pause of prayer,
when all my rushing thoughts descend
suddenly toward a silence, where
turmoil and turbulency end

in a deep inward quietness—
my thoughts race thither and are still.
Prayer is mind's millpond, whence I press
forth with fresh power to turn life's mill.

Prayer Is Life

I have made many kinds of prayer, almost wordless prayers of spiritual anguish, and formal prayers learned by rote. I have prayed on waking in the morning, in the evening as I have fallen asleep, and at special times I have set aside by day. I have joined in prayer with others, said grace at meals, recited psalms in church. Waking at night, I have prayed alone. In my times of deepest need I have prayed, and I have prayed when I had no need except to feel at one with God—though this may be the deepest need of all.

Prayer has meant so much to me that I have wondered how those who do not pray are sometimes able to survive. What do they do when there is nothing they can do?

Prayer is survival power. Though the night may come down dark around and the faith with which we face the night seem small, perhaps no faith at all; yet, if we pray, always some spark leaps up through the tinder of our hearts, a little light to show us our way. Prayer is life.

Prayer is a reaching, and every act of prayer stretches the soul. Prayer is spiritual exercise.

There are many ways to pray, as there are many ways to God. The way of the bird is not the way of the fish. The way of the babe is not the way of the adult. The way of the beginner is not the way of the master. Yet there is no atom of creation that does not have access to God. Each soul finds its way to God at the level of its own experience.

For some, prayer is thought; and for some, it is feeling too inarticulate for thought to express. Communion with nature may be prayer, or the enjoyment of art and poetry and music. An act of kindness may be a prayer, a smile, a friendly hand. Work is often a prayer, for work is an affirmation of creative power. Praise is a kind of prayer. So is zeal. There is the prayer that is the distillation of a moment, passionate and intense, and the prayer that is the whole life of a man, the living prayer of what one is.

There is a prayer that is words,

and a prayer that is silence. To rise, the eagle sometimes has to drive with all its pinioned power; and sometimes, launching itself on an updraft of air, it has only to spread its wings and float serenely in order to be borne aloft.

Sometimes when I pray I pray aloud. To control my thinking, I must often phrase my thoughts in words and speak the words aloud or even write them down. My thoughts may be likened to horses, milling in my mind, racing this way and that; but words put a bridle on them and enable me to direct them. So I often have to affirm words of Truth over and over in order to direct my thought Godward.

Yet sometimes when I pray I do not need to speak any word at all. I merely need to turn my thought to God, and the thought of God floods my mind. I merely need to give myself to God, and God gives Himself to me.

Much of prayer is speaking, yet much of it is listening. And the speaking we do in prayer is important, but the listening is even more important. For it is as we listen that God speaks. And it is when we are still that God acts. It is in the silence that the word of God is uttered and the work of God is done.

Some wonder how they will recognize the word of God. I know only that when God speaks it is in a language you will understand. If it is words, it will be words you know. If it is feelings, you will understand them too. For feeling is the unforgotten language of the heart; you could speak it before you learned words, the language of the mind.

There is a prayer that asks for things and a prayer that asks for thoughts, and there is a prayer that asks for nothing but gives all. I have prayed for many things. I have cried aloud for help; I have wheedled and bargained and demanded—but what have I ever really prayed for except to know that I am a child of God? I have seen the beautiful bird of Truth fly overhead and would hold it in my heart.

I would know God and understand my relation to God, and I would know God and know myself, not with an intellectual knowing, but in every fiber of my mind and heart. And this is why I pray.

For this is a knowing that does not come from study, but only from prayer. There are many kinds of knowing. Sometimes the mind studies life as it studies a book; it skims over the surface and absorbs not life, but words, which it calls life.

It is one thing to read a book on aerodynamics; it is another thing to fly. As a bird knows flight by flying, I would know life by living. And I would know God, not as a word, but as a living presence in my life.

I am the green plant of God, and I would know God as the leaves of a tree know sunlight. I would absorb God and be absorbed in God. I would make God's substance mine and His life mine so that I can make my life and substance His. I would use God to be used by Him.

This is why I pray.

Many times when I have prayed for things, I have not gotten what I prayed for, yet I feel I have never prayed in vain.

Perhaps things have not changed as I have wished them to change, but always I have changed. Always some change is wrought by prayer, sometimes in the fabric of things, always in the fabric of self.

Then, too, I have a sense that my life is more than I have power to see or foresee.

Columbus was disappointed in his search for India—and discovered a new world! I, too, have been disappointed in this or that—and have discovered new worlds. My own Self is such a world. God is such a world.

Prayer is a journey we make

Prayer is survival power. Though the night may come down dark around and the faith with which we face the night seem small, perhaps no faith at all; yet, if we pray, always some spark leaps up through the tinder of our hearts, a little light to show us our way. Prayer is life.

into ourselves, a journey we make toward God. We think of ourselves as islands, but we are truly mainlands. Beyond the cape of self lies a continent of being. It is not to our changing mortal self that we must look to understand our meaning and our destiny, but to this larger selflessness that lies beyond. "For this corruptible must put on incorruption, and this mortal must put on immortality" (1 Cor. 15:53 KJV).

The highest prayer is not the one that asks for things, but the one that seeks a sense of God and our relation to God, a sense of our abiding in the hands of God, in the love of God.

The prayer that is answered is the prayer of the whole human being. What our whole being demands—this is what we always receive from life; it may or may not be what we cry out for in a moment of pain or desire.

This is why prayer often works in great needs more readily than in trivial ones. A great need focuses the whole of us, whets us, as it were, to a razor edge of faith that nothing can resist.

Prayer is the marshaling of all our faculties. It is a unifying force. Sometimes we feel like "splinter" people, lonely and alone. We cannot read our direction right. But prayer orients us. It unifies us with

ourselves and makes us whole. It unifies us with life and makes us alive. It unifies us with God.

Prayer is not for the purpose of changing things but of changing us. It is not to make the Infinite conform to our will but to help us understand and conform to the will of the Infinite. Shall I change the sea by shouting or the wind by wailing? Yet when I was a child I dug a hole in the sand; and even as I dug, the sea welled into the hole and filled it full. When I pray I dig down through the sands of self, so that the sea of God may fill me full.

I do not pray to change God. How would I change the wholly good? The breeze of God blows steady all the time; I pray so that I may avail myself of it.

It is not God but I who needs to change. This is why I use affirmative prayer.

At the center of things there is a harmonious will. This will is life; this will is joy; this will is order; this will is love. Affirmative prayer harmonizes us with this central will of being.

This is affirmative prayer—to know in the face of sickness that underneath are the everlasting arms of wholeness and in the truest part of us we are inseparably one with life; to be able to hear

It is not God but I who needs to change. **This is why I use affirmative prayer.** At the center of things there is a harmonious will. This will is life; this will is joy; this will is order; this will is love. Affirmative prayer harmonizes us with this central will of being.

through the discords of daily living the music of immortal love and to strike its chords from the key of our own being; to be able to look at lack, yet to drink deep from unseen wells of plenty. It is the ability to see the facts and flaws, yet know that they are not reality.

True prayer is apprehension of the changeless Truth, which abides at the heart of the changeful world, the Truth of life and joy and order and love, the Truth of God.

For myself, I have not found the meaning and value of prayer to lie so much in the answer to prayer as in the prayer itself. For prayer is a way of life as well as a way of facing life. It is an end as well as a means. It is a spiritual experience.

Prayer is the way of walking with God instead of walking alone. Those who have a habit of prayer are never far from God, even though at times they may lose sight of God.

Because they have the habit of prayer, they often find things changed by their prayers. But even when things do not change they have a sense that all is well. For they have a sense of a sustaining presence—at the heart of things, compassion!

Though they may not understand why some things occur, they know that God is there. Therefore, nothing that occurs can be meaningless. They and their lives are meaningful.

So they can accept their lives and themselves, striving to change what they feel is good to change, but accepting what they cannot change in the faith that behind all the events of life God is working out His pattern of divinity.

To those who pray, prayer is life itself!

Nothing Can Be Possessed

I said to the Master, "Tell me about things. Is it wrong to pray for things?"

The Master said, "It is wrong not to pray for things. If prayer is right, then there is no aspect of living that we should not pray about.

"Pray about things, and you will find that you have the things you need, and you have also the attitude toward things you need."

Then I thought about things.

I saw that it is futile to pray for the possession of things, for things can never be possessed.

Nothing can be possessed. We have the use of things, but we never have the possession of them, however many titles to them we may deposit with the recorder of deeds, however many locks and strongboxes we may use for hiding them. There is nothing that is ours to keep. Not one thing. Sooner or later, we will have to give it away or it will be taken away. Everything. Even our body. Even our mind. Everything was the gift of life. And life asks it back. According to the greatest teacher of all,

life asks it back with interest; life expects it to have grown under our care. Life asks what we have done with what was given us. Have we turned it into a trash heap, or into a park?

Life is for us to be alive in.

Life is not to build a castle on. A castle is a vast pile of stones, damp, gloomy, and usually uncomfortable. After a short time, nobody wants to live there anymore; then it becomes a ruin.

Life is to grow a garden in. A garden lives. A garden grows. A garden changes a bare patch of land into a place of trees and flowers and grass and fountains splashing into pools and singing birds and buzzing insects.

Life is not a thing of stones for stones, but a thing alive for things alive—for mayflies and pine trees and hummingbirds, and you and me.

A gardener knows what a garden is like. A gardener knows that no one possesses a garden.

No one owns the land. In a well-built house the landlord is merely a lodger—with rooms for a week, a year, five years, fifty years. Generations of mockingbirds sing in the branchtops. Generations of moles tunnel the lawns, smelling out the grubs that live here too. The rabbits mock at the fences; the pokeweed lords it in the lot corner; the flower garden belongs no more to the gardener than to the bees that sup the flowers. In the limestone of the walls are the remains of shellfish that swam here once, and perhaps … the gardener is content to plant his trees and not trouble himself as to who will lie in their shade.

Not for Forever

Till the ground, tend the plant, pluck the flower as you wish. But the garden grows with spring and rests with fall.

You may take the flower, dry it, and place it in a glass case—but it is not the flower. You have only a bit of colored straw, slowly fading, slowly powdering. Keep it long enough and you will have only colorless dust.

Things are not for forever.

Things are like smiles and frowns that flit across the face of the Eternal. When a smile becomes fixed, it turns into a grimace. When a frown becomes fixed, it is just another wrinkle.

To enjoy things is not to possess them or to be possessed by them, but to use them. The joy of anything is the use of it. The joy of anything is to take it and make it into something more.

Rows of dresses hanging dusty in a closet, dresses no one wears any longer; tools slowly rusting in a tool shed, where no one comes to work; books that have gotten yellow and brittle with age because no loving hand ever fondles them or opens their pages; or a house in which no one has lived for a long time—there are few things sadder than these.

The joy is not to have a shining plane in your tool chest, but to take the plane out and plane a board with it until the board is flat and smooth and true.

To do this is to know what things are for.

The joy is not to have a beautiful dress in your closet, but to wear the dress to make the day or evening colorful and bright and interesting to you and your friends—or even to give it away when you will not wear it.

The joy is not to have a book upon a shelf, neat and perfect in its shining clean dust jacket, but to read the book and rejoice in its information or its inspiration, even to scribble in its margin—or to lend it to friends to read, even friends who never return it.

It is right to pray for things. When you pray, pray knowing that life lavishes its things, crowding every crack of space with its fecund living stuff, pressing into every outstretched hand its over-flowing bounty.

Know, too, that things are not for forever. Things are not to hold on to. Hold on long enough and you will wish you had cast even the dearest thing away.

There is a great Japanese myth. It is about twin deities, Izanagi and Izanami, who were devoted lovers and produced the Japanese islands and their people. When Izanami died in childbirth, the sorrowing Izanagi could not let her go but followed her into the underworld begging her to return to him. When he neared her in the darkness, she asked him not to look at her, for she knew that death had not made her sightly. But he lit the comb that held his hair in place, and saw her moldering.

Clutch things to you, and when life comes round again, where will it leave its gifts? For whatever you have, life has yet more to give.

The snake must slough its skin; the bird must molt its feathers; and the evergreen that lives for a thousand years must give up many of its boughs as it grows.

Is the corn less because it gives itself for food?

Or the Sun because it gives itself for light?

Things are made for life, not life for things. Pray for them, knowing that they are yours to use, to enjoy, and to expend—for the increase of your own joy-in-living and for the joy-in-life of others.

for his own saf...
complaineth of their wro...
Psalm of Dā'vid.

...cause, O LORD,
...strive with me;

...ight
...me.

...knew it
and cease...
16 With
feasts,
their f...

X.

Jesus

O Lord, Whose Very Name Is Love

Jesus Savior, little stranger,
you were cradled in a manger.
Could it be, then, as you grew,
there were no questionings in you?
Did you have no thoughts like me,
no doubts of your divinity?
Feel no inward ache to know?
Never have the need to grow?
When you went to pray apart,
was it with no puzzled heart?
O Lord, whose very name is love
made flesh, O incarnation of
infinite compassion, can
You, being God, be less than man?
You had no splendor like a king's.
I see you in the least of things;
I see you shining through man's tears,
through his uncertainties and fears.
O holy infant, little stranger,
here is my heart—be it your manger!

The One We All Might Be

There was One who showed us what we all might be. He did not so much tell us what our lives should be like, he lived the life that we might live.

The One we all might be had faith in other people. He saw in them potentialities that others overlooked. He knew them to be capable of more than they themselves thought. He inspired sinners to become saints, social outcasts to become public benefactors, weaklings to become towers of strength. He changed common fishermen into "fishers of men."

The One we all might be saw through life's imperfections—through sickness and doubt, through poverty and fear, through hatred and pride, even through death—and he called forth wholeness, faith, joy, love, and life. He showed us what life might be—lived to the utmost of its possibilities. He showed us what a person might be who held to the highest and best in himself.

How hard we find it to love one or two persons! Yet he showed us that it is possible to learn to love all. How many hours we have wasted in resentment! Yet this One showed us that it is possible to live free from hate.

He knew how much a loving heart is worth, he had a sense of right values. He was able to judge not by appearances; able to put first things first; able to see how much more important than material treasures are the treasures of heart and mind.

He saw people as they are, flesh-and-blood creatures with physical needs and desires. Not once did he suggest, "It will be better for your soul if your body suffers, so I will not help you." Those who were sick, he healed; those who were hungry, he fed. He knew that love does not exact pain-payments as the price of spiritual growth.

This is no man of sorrows, though he wept. Though he suffered, his was no tragic life. Even his death was not truly tragic, for how quickly the darkness of Calvary was wiped away in the light of Easter morning! The energy released by the overcoming that he made at death is still flooding, two thousand years later, into millions of lives.

His was no easy life, but surely people are not given their tremendous mental and spiritual powers in order to have a problem-free existence.

This One had human needs and human problems. Had he not been endowed with human nature, then he could not have meant to us what he means. We could not aspire to put on his character. We could not hope to imitate his life. Though this be "very God of very God," this is also "very man of very man."

How human was his love for his family! Almost his last act, as he hung on the cross, was to commit his mother to the care of his best friend.

He was weary, and he rested by the well. He was thirsty, and he said, "Give me a drink" (Jn. 4:10). He was angered at people's inability to see the Truth—though never at the people themselves—and he expressed his anger in flaming words and sometimes in hot deeds. When he saw the sadness of his friends, he wept. He shrank from pain as all people do. He cried, "Remove this cup from me," though he added, "Not my will but yours be done" (Lk. 22:42).

He had moments of doubt and cried out like a child, "My God, my God, why have you forsaken me?" (Mt. 27:46)

Yet he was intimately aware of his oneness with God. He was human, but always he saw himself as more than a human being; he saw himself as a spiritual being with spiritual powers.

He fed people with bread when they needed it; he healed their bodies and minds. But he knew also that we cannot live by bread alone, we must have the living bread of inspiration, and this he offered never-ceasingly.

He saw life clear and saw it whole, and he saw himself as part of the whole, just as he knew that the whole was part of him. He saw that in the truest sense he and the whole were one. He could say to those who would see God to look at him.

Here was no splinter of a man, lonely or afraid, wondering as to his meaning and function in the vastness of the universe. This One knew that all of us are one with one another and with the whole.

He knew the Truth about himself, not in abstract words but in every fiber of his being. He was so conscious of his Godlikeness that he was never anything less.

He was aware of his spiritual power. He called forth no armies of angels, caused no signs to be displayed in the heavens, but al-

The One we all might be saw through life's imperfections—through sickness and doubt, through poverty and fear, through hatred and pride, even through death—and he called forth wholeness, faith, joy, love, and life.

He showed us what life might be—lived to the utmost of its possibilities. He showed us what a person might be who held to the highest and best in himself.

ways he was the master of himself and of powers beyond himself.

This One was able to focus all the energies that we dissipate on trivialities, fears, and hatred on whatever problem was presented to him; and before the fierce heat of his spiritual power the problem was melted away.

Was there a multitude to be fed? With what was at hand the need was met.

Was there one who was dumb or blind, one who was lame or mad? "The blind receive their sight, the lame walk, the lepers are cleansed, and the deaf hear, the dead are raised" …. (Lk. 7:22)

Even over death he had power, for he knew that in truth death has no power or reality. Though he died, it was only to rise again.

So great was the power this One laid hold of that whatever he was called on to meet, whether for himself or another, he met victoriously.

Yet even in his use of power he taught us much. Though this One was the most powerful one who ever lived, he was also the most responsible. There is no instance when he used his power to force another to do his will. This was no Zeus hurling thunderbolts at his enemies. When the people of his hometown tried to mob him, he did not call down angels to defend him; he slipped quietly away.

The One we all might be showed us how humble true greatness is!

He could be humble because he understood his worth. "Who do you say that I am?" (Mt. 16: 15) he asked his Apostles, and Peter's answer rings across a score of centuries, "You are the Messiah, the Son of the living God" (Mt. 16: 16). Knowing who he was, he did not have to puff himself up with titles and pretense. He could wash the feet of his friends. He could mix with the lowliest and the least worthy, with no awareness of their lowliness or their unworthiness. Neither do I condemn thee, he said.

Yet he had an unfailing sense of his own worth. He let his feet be bathed in precious ointments. Even when he appeared as a criminal on trial for his life, he had such poise that he unnerved the Roman dignitary, Pilate.

He was meek, not weak. He avoided quarrels when he could; but when he had to engage in argument, his wit shone like a sword. His was the meekness that springs from the awareness of strength; his was the humility that springs from the awareness of worth.

He was filled with spiritual light, but he had great practical wisdom too. He had an infinite understanding of people and of the springs of action in them. He saw the causes of unhappiness, and he knew the way to happiness. He knew that every idle word that men shall speak, they shall give account thereof. He knew that it is not enough for people to control their actions, they must control their thinking too. He believed in obeying laws, but he repeatedly reminded his friends that laws were made for men, and not men for laws.

He was as much a man of action as he was a man of faith and love. Though he was always in close communion with his Father, though he spent days and nights and even weeks in prayer and meditation, he knew that heaven had to be established not only in mind and heart but also had to be made a living reality in the physical universe.

He did not withdraw from the world, nor did he allow his apostles to withdraw. He sent them out, not to meditate but to preach the gospel to the poor ... to heal the brokenhearted, to preach deliverance to the captives and recovering of sight to the blind, to set at liberty them that are bruised.

He was without fear for personal safety, without worry about personal needs, for he knew that all the powers of the universe work together for those who are in harmony with them. Life clothed the lilies of the field and cared for the sparrows—why should he fear? He was not concerned as to whether what he did was financially profitable, only as to whether it was profitable to humankind. He was concerned only with the Truth.

He did not lack for shelter, though he had nowhere to lay his head. He could say to the storm, "Peace! Be still!" (Mk. 4:39) The waves could not sweep away his clear, sure calm. Serene in his purpose, he never lost his sense of direction.

This One embodied what we only envision. But however nobler than our own his character may be, however superior to our own his powers may seem, however larger than our own his accomplishments may loom, this is what we all might be. His is the life we all might live.

Certainly this One believed this to be true.

"Follow me," (Lk. 9:59) he said. "The one who believes in me will also do the works that I do and, in fact, will do greater works than these" (Jn. 14:12). "All things are possible to him who believes" (Mk. 9:23 RSV).

This is God in incarnation, as we are God in aspiration. When Principle incarnates in human form, this is the kind of life that results. But Principle is incarnate in all of us. This is the life toward which all of us are moving. It is our own faces that look down at us from Calvary, and it is in our own flesh that we feel the stir of Easter morning. He knew this, and he said, "I in them and you in me, that they may become completely one" (Jn. 17:23).

What height of fulfillment, what depth of compassion, what breadth of understanding might be ours—if we were all that we might be!

Ours to love with a love that excludes none but gives itself to all.

To have a sense of right values, placing spiritual things first, yet using spiritual powers to transform the physical world.

To be master of self and superior to circumstance.

To be humble of spirit, yet conscious of eternal worth.

To be at peace, yet to be a center of energy.

To be God-centered, a focus through which His power flows freely in joyous achievement.

To be unlimited in vision and to attain what we envision.

To experience the fullness of compassion, yet to live to the fullness of joy.

To be able to help all who turn to us, to bless the lives we touch, to turn sorrow into joy, hate into love, sickness into health, lack into fulfillment, death into life.

To be one with the essential harmony at the center of things.

To be free from worry and fear about our physical necessities in the faith that this is a hospitable universe.

To see ourselves in relation to the whole, merging the fraction of self in the integer of God!

This is what we all might be.

There Was Once a Man of Love

There was once a man of love. He went around the country helping people and teaching them to love one another.

When he met people who were sick, he told them, "You weren't meant to be sick like this. You are the child of love, and love made you. Can you believe that? Then you know that love wouldn't make you to be sick."

When he came on people who were poor, he told them, "You weren't meant to be poor, you were meant to be rich. You are the child of love. Love made the world, and it made a beautiful world with plenty in it for everybody. Can you believe that you are the child of love?"

When he saw people who were unhappy, he told them, "You weren't meant to be unhappy. Love made you. And could love have meant anything for you but happiness? Then believe that you are the child of love and claim your happiness!"

And the people who believed that what he said made sense got a new vision of themselves and their world. The people who were sick were made whole, and the people who were poor found the means to meet their needs, sometimes even in a fish's mouth. And the people who were unhappy began to sing songs in praise of love and of life.

But the people who ran the world did not like what they heard when they heard what this man was saying. If people began to live by love, what need would there be for kings and judges? And even if they still got to run the world, if they had to run it as if it were the kind of world love has made, they didn't know how.

So they got together and decided they had to do something about this smooth love talk and this soft love talker. "He's a public enemy," they told one another. "He'd overthrow all the existing institutions, and that would include us. This man would even abolish death and taxes; he's an atheist anarchist, that's what he is, and we'd be untrue to our responsibilities if we didn't take steps to save the world from his false teaching."

Then they put all their heads

close together and they thought, How can we catch him?

The people who ran the world were not sure who the man of love was, he was so much like every man. That's the way it is with love, it makes you like those you love. And this man was so filled with love that he was hardly separate from anyone. Since he loved everyone, he had come to look like everyone else and his love brought him so close to those he loved that it was almost as if he were an inseparable part of them.

Then one of the people who ran the world had a bright idea. He said, "We can catch him through his love."

So they found someone he loved and paid him a sum of money to betray him. They said to him, "All you have to do is, when you find him, kiss him. He'll like you to do that because he loves you." Then they all fell to laughing because they thought this was such a clever way to catch the man of love—with a kiss. "That will teach him what love will do for

And the people who believed that what he said made sense got a new vision of themselves and their world. The people who were sick were made whole, and the people who were poor found the means to meet their needs, sometimes even in a fish's mouth. And the people who were unhappy began to sing songs in praise of love and of life.

you," they told one another.

So that night the one he loved went up to him and kissed him, and those who ran the world, who had been slinking about in the bushes, came clanking up in their armor and seized him.

Some of his friends wanted to make a fight of it, but the man of love said to them sadly, "Is it for this that I have loved you?" Then they dropped their swords and went away quietly.

When those who ran the world had the man of love, they began shuttling him back and forth among themselves, each one saying to the other, "I think you're the one to take care of this," and each one trying to wash his hands of the matter—for who wants to be responsible for killing love? They expected him to get angry and curse them and create a disturbance, so that they could have a proper court trial. But all he did was look at them with eyes of love, and all he said was: "I love you. I love you all, no matter what you do."

Finally they had him taken out and hanged. They hanged him on a cross instead of a gallows, because that is what they used in those days; it hurt more. But it didn't take him long to die, which those who ran the world thought was just as well. After he was dead, in a move to pacify any hard feelings, they let his friends cut him down and bury him.

But a few days later, rumors began to creep about the town. It was being said that the man of love they had hanged was still out there hanging. Their spies came and told them this.

"But that's impossible," said those who ran the world. "We had him taken down and buried."

"That may be," said the spies, "but the report we get is that he's still up there hanging high."

"Maybe we'd better go look," said those who ran the world. They weren't sure where to look, but they decided if he was anywhere, he would probably be where his friends were, and sure enough, there they found the man of love, hanging up there high for anyone to see.

"We can see if you want something done right, you have to do it yourself," they said. "And we've certainly got to put an end to this man of love."

For one thing, they knew in their heart that what they had done was a shameful deed and they wanted to hide it from themselves. And for a more practical reason, the last thing they wanted was for the man of love to be left hanging there to become a subject of general concern.

So this time they cut him down and buried him themselves. But in a few days, their spies were back again, saying, "More and more people are saying more and more, he is still up there hanging."

Then the reports that he was up there hanging began to come in from all sorts of places. The rulers of the world were beside themselves. Every time they came on him up there hanging, they cut him down and buried him. "Why doesn't he stay buried like any respectable, law-abiding citizen would?" they asked one another. But he just didn't.

At last they became so angry they decreed that anybody who even reported they had seen him up there hanging would be hanged themselves. This caused them to

They knew in their heart that what they had done was a shameful deed and they wanted to hide it from themselves. And for a more practical reason, the last thing they wanted was for the man of love to be left hanging there to become a subject of general concern. So this time they cut him down and buried him themselves. But in a few days, their spies were back again, saying, "More and more people are saying more and more, he is still up there hanging."

hang a lot of people. But in spite of all the hangings, more and more people kept claiming they had seen the man of love up there hanging; and more and more people began to wonder and ask, "Is it possible no one can kill the man of love?"

I wonder myself.

For men are still cutting down the man of love that they hanged and are still trying to bury him and keep him buried. But he is still up there hanging, no matter how many times they cut him down, no matter how many times they bury him. And from what I can see, he is hanging in more human hearts and more human minds and more human lives all the time. More and more human beings throughout the Earth are asking, "Is it possible that what the man of love has tried to tell us is true? That the world was made by love, and we are the children of love. And we can live by love and bring forth a world of beauty and health and plenty and happiness, where we can all dwell together free from hate and fear and selfishness and be the beloved men and women of love."

As I say, I wonder.

For the man of love, after all these centuries, is still up there hanging high, and that's a beautiful and serene smile I see on his face.

I think the time is not far off when the man of love will no longer have to be up there hanging. He will be down here, walking every street, doing every task, meeting every need, transforming every life. As I said, we come to look like what we love; that's why the man of love looks like everyone. But the time is not far off when everyone will look like him.

XI.

Humankind

If Thoughts Had Shapes

If thoughts had shapes like things,
I wonder what they'd be—
would wonder not be wings
and reverie a sea?

If hope looked like a seed,
would lilies grow for grace,
would worry be a weed,
despair a barren space?

Would thoughts of Truth not find
a rainbow's radiant form,
and would not peace of mind
be sunlight after storm?

And love, what shape would show
love patient, warm, and true?
All you I love, I know
that love would look like you.

189

Immortal Journey

What am I? What am I doing here? Where am I going?

I have a print by the Spanish artist Goya called El Colosso, the Colossus. A huge naked brute of a fellow is sitting on a log looking up at the Moon and stars—his face full of question. Many times I have felt like El Colosso.

Emerson said, "What I have seen teaches me to trust my Creator for what I have not seen," and for the most part, I have been content to do that. Life has brought me up to here. For all its aches and challenges, I have found it livable and sometimes even lovable. As to where I came from, and where I am going after this life, I have not worried much as to particulars.

Personally, I find it impossible to accept the traditional notions about heaven and hell. Heaven and hell are real enough as states of mind—I have known people in both. But to believe in hell as an actual place where living souls are tortured eternally, you have to believe in a crueler God than I believe it possible for God to be.

I once had a vivid vision of hell. I was outraged at the thought that the God of love whom I love could create such a place. But as the demon dragged me down into it, he said: "You don't have the right idea about this place. It's only here because you need it. If you'll look around, you'll see there is no one here except the people you think ought to be here."

As to heaven, I pray that we may one day attain it, but perfect bliss would require utter selflessness and perfect love. It is pretty obvious that if we should get into it now, heaven would not stay heavenly long.

Whatever else life—present or future—may contain, it must contain change. The one essential element in life, the element that makes life alive, is change. To be what you and I are, here or elsewhere, is to change—and hopefully, to grow.

I believe we are immortal beings.
I am immortal, I aver,
For I must live as if I were.
Everyone feels immortal. The psychiatrist, Karl Menninger, has

said: "No human being can in the deepest core of his nature conceive of nonexistence or imagine it occurring to him."

Life does not make sense if this is all the life there is. It is too unjust, and I believe in a God who is just. Even more. God is justice. God is law. God is even the law that is love.

Hundreds and hundreds of persons have had experiences that have convinced them that life goes on beyond this one. Such an experience is individual and subjective; you cannot make it come real to anyone who has not had it. But if you ever have one—this I know— it will be the most real thing that ever happens to you.

We are on an immortal journey. Children of the eternal, we are making a voyage in time, and we have come up to here.

As to the particulars of our voyage, I suppose I believe in something like reincarnation. Reincarnation seems comparatively reasonable, though personally, I don't like the word; it turns people off.

Many years ago I was studying French at the Convent of Notre Dame de Sion. The nun who taught me was a very intelligent woman, a graduate of the Sorbonne. She liked to argue with me about religion. Since the arguments were in French, I always lost. But the arguments were fun. When I brought her a piece about reincarnation, she rejected it as being utterly beyond belief. Finally, I said: "What do you believe? Do you think you go sit on a cloud somewhere with a harp?" "Of course not," she said indignantly. "I believe that life is a continuous process and progress." I laughed and said, "You aren't rejecting the idea of reincarnation, you are rejecting the word, because all that reincarnation does is suggest how the process and progress may occur."

Most of the world believes in reincarnation; most of it always has. The East has always accepted the idea as the most reasonable that has ever been suggested; and though it has not been the prevailing belief in the West, thousands of famous and intelligent people from Plato and Plotinus to Edison and Einstein have believed in it.

An amazing number of people do. General Patton—he hardly seems the type to be bowled over by mystical notions—was absolutely convinced he had been a soldier many times.

Many people, like Patton, have believed that reincarnation

humankind

takes place here on Earth over and over. As for myself, I believe God's house has many rooms in it. I believe I have lived before. I believe I will live again. As to where and how, perhaps it will be here—I love this blue-green glowing globe—perhaps it will be beyond space and even time, an inverted world where thoughts are things and things are thoughts. But since it will have me in it, it will not be too different, because I cannot be too different and still be me. The essential will remain essentially the same.

Does the thought that you have lived many times seem strange to you? How many lives have you lived in this one? When I was ten years old, my whole life changed absolutely and altogether. My mother ran away from her marriage and took me and my sister fifteen hundred miles from everything and everyone we knew. Everybody who had been in my former life was gone, except my mother and sister. And all the circumstances and conditions changed utterly.

Of my life when I was ten, or even twenty, what remains? The people who were close are scattered across the Earth or gone from it.

When I was thirty-one, I had a tremendous spiritual experience. After agonizing soul-searching, I came to such an illumining realization about myself, I have often told friends that I count my true birth as from that time. I went through a gate of awareness, and life on a different plane of sensitivity began.

When I was thirty-five, I lost my first wife. That was the end of a life too; a whole new set of people and experiences came into it.

When I was fifty-five, I began yet another new life. I started to travel and speak. Since then my life experiences have altered radically again.

And I have lived these different lives, although I have lived in one city since I was ten and have done one work since I was seventeen.

What about you? How many who were an important part of your life, say at twenty, are still an important part of your life? Or when you were ten? Or at your birth? Of those important to you when you were born—a very important moment—how many are important to you still? Very, very few, I would say. Even if you are very young, very few, probably.

People accompany us on this immortal journey, some for a long

192

time and some but briefly. Their importance in our lives does not depend on how long they are with us. They can be with us for an hour—less than that, for minutes—and be transformingly important!

A few years ago I made some talks in Palm Beach. On my last day there, I spoke at a nursing home. After I made my talk, a nurse came up to me and said: "There is a woman who has asked to see you. Could you come and see her? She is very near death." She led me down a long hall and into a room where a woman lay in bed. The moment I walked into that room, I knew why I had come to Palm Beach. It had not been to make the speeches I had made. It had been because this woman

Hundreds and hundreds of persons have had experiences that have convinced them that life goes on beyond this one. Such an experience is individual and subjective; you cannot make it come real to anyone who has not had it. But if you ever have one—this I know—it will be the most real thing that ever happens to you.
We are on an immortal journey.
Children of the eternal,
we are making a voyage in time,
and we have come up to here.

had drawn me there. Don't ask me how, I don't know, but I knew that woman I had never seen before in this lifetime—I don't even know her name—as well as I have ever known anybody in this life, better than people I have known for years and years. There is no question in my mind, that woman and I for a moment had to reestablish our relationship (don't ask me what it was, I do not know, but I know that it was there and very strong) before she could go on. And so she called me to her—and I went.

People say, "I can't believe I have lived before, because I can't remember anything about those lives." But how much do you remember about this one? Very little. On this date ten years ago, where were you? I haven't the slightest idea where I was. On this date last year, where was I? I don't know. Do you know where you were? And if by accident you happen to remember the events of that particular day, do you remember where you were a week before that? Or a month before? Whom you were with and what you were doing?

And when you were ten years old, what do you remember of that year? That was one of the most eventful years in my life. But I have to think and think for a few events to dribble faintly back into my mind. And of the time when you were five? If you can recall anything, is it not usually because someone later told you it had happened?

And when we were four, three, two, one? Can we remember anything?

One time my grandfather introduced me to Buffalo Bill. That was an occasion! But now my grandfather and Buffalo Bill and King Arthur and Robin Hood are all mixed up together in my mind. The most vivid events of my life are much like something I read in a book.

The past has an unreality about it. A mist falls between us and the past, and the mist deepens quickly, so the figures that move in it through our minds become but phantasms, doubtful and indistinct; which is figure and which is mist becomes harder and harder to make out.

Time writes. But also it erases—almost as fast as it writes. We think of time as a rope with the events of our lives tied like knots along its length. But this is not what time is like. Time is like a bunch of keepsakes we have tossed into a drawer of our minds. There they lie tangled together. We may pull them out for a moment, but after a while we forget just when it was we threw them in.

If you have known many older people, you have probably known some who at last could not remember anything about this life. They let it all go and slipped back, as it were, beyond their birth. I have often wondered, are they doing on this side of the door what we all must do when we pass through it?

We make our journey through time, but how strange time is. Time is important; we cannot even imagine anything happening without its taking time. But time is hard to fix or grasp. Rubbery and relative, it stretches or compresses, according to what is happening and who it is happening to and even where it is happening, conforming to all sorts of immeasurables of consciousness.

People have asked me, "If we are reborn, how long a time passes between incarnations?" I have often thought, perhaps no time at all—not in the sense of time as we mark it in the world of thoughts and things we spend this lifetime in.

Even when we are wide awake, time plays all kinds of tricks on us. A minute may be interminable; a

year may flash by. Have you never waited for some joyful or some dreadful event and counted not the seconds but the millionths of seconds? And have you never been so absorbed in some task that at last you glanced up and wondered where the day could have gone?

At night you often live in a different kind of time, the time in dreams, that has almost no relation to waking time. My friend Eric Butterworth once told me that one night he was driving a car down a country road and a hundred or so yards ahead of him he saw a stone bridge. At that moment he fell asleep, and in his sleep, he dreamed a dream the events of which took days to occur. Yet he woke almost instantly, for fortunately the car had not yet even reached the bridge.

And in deep sleep, does time have any meaning to us then? If it were not for clocks and the sun, would we know that it has passed? Is it more than a bodily process? Had it not been for his long beard, would Rip van Winkle have known that he had slept for twenty years?

Time is a measure of here and now. It is futile and perhaps meaningless to ask where it has gone or when it will be.

People sometimes tell me they don't like the idea of reincarnation because they want to recognize their dear ones. So do I, and I think I will. I always have.

But how? Do I expect my grandfather to be an old man with a walrus mustache—I think he had one—who will come up to me and say, "I'm Jim Elberson." And what will I be? The little ten-year-old he knew? I don't think he would like to be that old man, and I know I wouldn't like to be that ten-year-old. And my grandmother, his wife, might like it even less. She would want my grandfather and herself to be the young couple I never knew.

No, my grandfather is never again going to be the old man he was when I knew him, nor will I ever again be that little boy. Yet I hope to see my grandfather again somewhere in my journeys. And when we meet, I think we will recognize each other. How? The same way I have recognized my dear ones in this life.

How do I recognize my dear ones? My present wife did not come to me with a sign, saying "I am your w-i-f-e." I think she knew that long before I became aware of it, but that is not the way she came. She from Louisiana, I from Delaware, came by separate, dif-

Time writes. But also it erases—almost as fast as it writes. We think of time as a rope with the events of our lives tied like knots along its length. But this is not what time is like. Time is like a bunch of keepsakes we have tossed into a drawer of our minds. There they lie tangled together. We may pull them out for a moment, but after a while we forget just when it was we threw them in.

ferent paths, and when we met, were drawn, not by some vague recollection, but by deep inward stirrings, a feeling of oneness and love. Each found the other dear— that is all.

Only blood relatives come announced, and they may or may not be dear. When you were little, your mother led you toward a big woman bending down above you, and your mother said, "This is your Aunt Agatha." And you let out a scream and fled behind your mother's skirt.

No, dear ones don't come wearing tags or with a certain name or look. They come being dear. And that is the way we recognize them—as someone dear, close, loved. No one has to tell us. Heart speaks to heart, and that is a language all of us understand. That is the way it always has been, that is the way it will always be, that is the only way it could be.

I do not want my growth arrested anywhere. If an angel came and said to me, "Choose the happiest, most beautiful moment of your life, and I will let you stay there always," I would say to that angel: "Get thee behind me. I want to live now—always only now. I want to be alive, and to be alive is to change and to grow."

We make an immortal journey. Through chance and change, by way of worlds forgotten and courses unremembered yet graven in my soul, I came here and I journey on.

This is the human condition.

I have risen on innumerable mornings.

I have slept through innumerable nights.

I have journeyed on innumerable journeys.

I have lived in familiar and unfamiliar worlds.

I have had brave and beautiful companions, lovely friends.

I shall have them yet again.

I have been weak and strong, wise and unwise.

Ordinary things are the house of the beautiful.

Usual life is the fullness of living.

Every child is a holy infant.

Every one of us is a child of God.

Now we call a few extraordinary happenings wonders and miracles, such as the works of Jesus.

We say they are miracles because we cannot explain them and cannot duplicate them.

But what can we explain and what can we duplicate?

What is an ordinary thing?

I do not want my growth arrested anywhere. If an angel came and said to me, "Choose the happiest, most beautiful moment of your life, and I will let you stay there always," I would say to that angel, "Get thee behind me. I want to live now—always only now. I want to be alive, and **to be alive is to change and to grow."**

Take a cherry tree, for instance: black boughs of winter; on those naked boughs—green leaves; among those green leaves—white and fragrant flowers; and when those flowers fall—red, red cherries glistening till the tree sparkles like a ruby crown, where singing birds light lightly with their songs. I have not even mentioned the taste of cherries baked in a pie! I can only say, what delightful ways God has of revealing Himself to us.

Or take the starry sky. Go out of doors tonight and look at it, the glittering night aflame with stars—not one so large as candlelight, still tapers, but with a power to move the spirit more than any summer fireworks show!

Or a baby!

Little Jesus, O Holy Infant, do we need to ask you if a baby is a wonder and a miracle?

If a genie suddenly materialized, we would be struck dumb with astonishment.

We see a child, a cherry, or a star. We are delighted, but we act as if these were not as great a marvel as a genie.

We have only to look inside ourselves or step outside our door to see ten thousand wonders, each one as implausible, unexplainable, and unique as a genie.

The fact that they are wonders that happen every day does not make them less wonderful. Nor does the fact that I can sometimes correctly predict that one of them may after awhile turn into another of them—a cherry stone into a cherry tree, for instance.

I cannot duplicate a single one of them. I cannot tell you how it came to be or what it is. I cannot tell you why it is, nor can the wisest scientist.

I might say, "God!" But the word is meaningful only if you have yourself found out its meaning.

All that I can say is that I see everywhere the work of creative Spirit.

Everything God makes is an original creation. God never mass-produces anything.

God did not turn you out on a machine. You are handmade. God did not make you like anyone else.

There are more than four billion human beings. No two of them are alike. Once in a while, almost as if in an excess of creativity—much like a grace note in a symphony—there are identical twins. But even these are different—and there are just enough of these to show that the Spirit that is at work is altogether unpredictable.

What Are We?

In the year 1781 the planet Uranus was discovered. Having discovered it, astronomers, peering with crude instruments across almost two billion miles of space computed the course in the heavens it would have to take. But after watching its movement for many years, they became aware that it was not following this course.

Two young men, a Frenchman named Urbain Leverrier and an English college student named John Couch Adams, neither aware of the work of the other, determined to figure out why. To do this, they did not turn a telescope on the skies. They went to work on the problem in their minds. And there, in their minds, without looking at the sky at all, they found the answer.

The only way to account for the deviation in the orbit of Uranus, they said, was that out beyond Uranus, there must be, undiscovered and unknown, yet another planet. Not only that, but this planet had to be in a certain spot in the heavens!

When the astronomers at the Berlin observatory turned their telescope on that spot, there, almost three billion miles away, too small for naked eye to see, no more than a drop of light in a telescope, right where the two young men had said it had to be, was the planet Neptune.

What are we? What is this mind of ours that through the power of thought can reach across the blind vasts of space, where eye has not penetrated, and declare what must be there? Or, in our own day, reaches down into the depthless abyss of the infinitesimal and, by manipulating imponderable particles that eye has never seen but mind declares must be there, releases unbelievable energies.

We are ourselves like Uranus. We think we know our nature and what may be expected of us. Then we discover that we do not know ourselves at all; we do not follow the predicted course. Beyond the Uranus of our conscious, sentient, reasoning nature—the "me" that eye can see and ear can hear—lies yet some farther Neptune that we must discover before we can say, "That am I."

What am I?

I am aware of my personal limitations. My inadequacies are plain enough. If I look without, I come quickly to my fingertips, my toenails, my hair. If I look within, I come quickly to the end of my knowledge. Beyond this little island stretch outer space and inner spacelessness.

Yet fire on the farthest outpost of the patriot's country, and you have fired on him. Where then does one stop? And where does one begin? Joan of Arc, burned at the stake, remained rational and calm, praying to the end.

Is this obvious fellow then— this conscious self I am usually so conscious of—what I really am? Is this my true Self? Or is this simply part of me, one aspect of me, as my hand is part of me, or my heart or the invisible wisdom that takes care of the manufacture of red blood cells in my bone marrow or that in me which flashes ideas into my conscious mind for it to form into a poem?

The truth is that I am not thought, not body, not passion, not feeling, not appetite, not emotion, not will, not conscious mind, not subconscious mind, not any of these things, nor all of them, but more.

I am not to be explained in psychological, nor economic, nor social, nor political, nor biological, nor religious terms. All of these explain aspects of my nature, but aspects only. Separately and altogether, they are not enough. I am yet more.

How much is a human being?

Mind can hold the heavens, all the galaxies that spangle space with stars, yet not be full. Is light swift? Thought can outstrip it. Who shall measure the height of mind or the depth of heart that can feel clear to the heart of being and know its oneness there with every living thing? And how shall we speak of our spirit save to say that it is one with the Spirit of God? As to our powers, when we consider what human beings have done, is there anything that we dare to put beyond them?

We converse across an ocean; we sit in San Francisco and watch events taking place in New York; we fly faster than sound; we cook without fire and cool without ice; we see through night and fog; we make our houses cool by summer and warm by winter and luminous by night; we probe the atom and put its power to work; we explore

We are ourselves like Uranus. **We think we know our nature** and what may be expected of us. Then we discover that we do not know ourselves at all; we do not follow the predicted course. Beyond the Uranus of our conscious, sentient, reasoning nature—the "me" that eye can see and ear can hear—lies yet some farther Neptune that we must discover before we can say, "That am I."

universes billions of light years distant; we heal disease; we lengthen life; we drain marshes and push back the sea; we make the desert bloom and the wilderness into a garden; we yoke the tides and waterfalls.

What are we that we should do all this?

What is a Mozart who writes a concerto at age eight? Or a Grandma Moses who paints a masterpiece at eighty? Or a Goethe who at eighteen or eighty-two produces inspired works?

Do you dare assert, "But I am not such as these"?

No one knows the strength of her body to do and bear, the reach of her mind to imagine and perceive, the capacity of her heart to love, the power of her spirit to change her world.

Is there anyone, even the most self-despising person, who has not sometime thought, I can't do that—and in the light of his past performance he could not do it—but then, suddenly he found that he was doing it?

I have seen men and women find healing when there seemed no way for them to be healed, and supply when there seemed no means of supply; and I have seen them bring peace to situations and to hearts where there seemed to be no hope but of war. I have seen them lose their possessions or their dear ones or suffer crippling illness, even blindness, and find that they had the resilience to meet the loss so that it became not the end of life but a new beginning. I have seen them keep on when they had nothing left except the spirit to keep on.

It is not only when I see a Mozart or a Grandma Moses that I sense greatness. I sense it when I look at anyone, even a beggar. For this, too, is life with all life's potentialities, with thoughts that may rise as high as Truth, longings that may reach as far as God, powers that may extend to the limits of faith. All this is there. I know it, and the better I get to know anyone, the more certainly I know it. Under the husks, there it is.

And everyone knows it too. For a beggar might change places with a king: change his rags for the king's robe, his ignorance for the king's knowledge, his weakness for the king's power—but his self for the king's self? Never. Why not? Because he knows deep down in his inmost reality, in the deep center of his being, in the real self of himself, "I am the very best that is!"

How shall anyone say of herself or another, "This am I, no more"? Did one do a deed? Another shall do as much and more. He who did most of all said, "The works that I do and, in fact, will do greater works than these" (Jn. 14:12). And he said, "If you have faith … nothing will be impossible for you" (Mt. 17:20).

One night outside of Houston, Texas, a truck crashed into a tree, pinning the driver, unconscious, in the twisted steel of the capsized cab, which caught fire. Two trucks were hooked to each end of the wreck to try to straighten it out so that the doors could be gotten open and the driver removed. This did not succeed. Men attacked the doors with crowbars but could not pry them open. Meanwhile, the fire reached the feet of the driver.

Then out of the dark stepped a man. He took hold of the door of the truck, which four trucks and men with crowbars had not been able to open, and he tore it from its hinges. He reached inside, bent back the steering wheel, plucked out of the floor as if they were straws the brake and clutch pedals in which the driver's feet were caught, and with his bare hands, beat out the flames.

Still they could not get the

driver out. So he wedged himself into the cab and began to straighten up. Those who were there said that they could hear the steel popping as the roof rose, and the man kept pushing up that steel roof till eager hands were able to reach in and remove the driver.

Without a word, the man disappeared then. But they found him a few days later. He was a black man named Charles Dennis Jones. When they asked him how he had been able to do what he had done, he said, simply, "You never know what you can do till you see another man hurting." It is not only Charles Dennis Jones who has power in him to help the hurting. It is every one of us.

The simple words of this man point the way to find this power in ourselves. It is to forget ourselves and think about others. To find ourselves we must lose ourselves. For we come to ourselves only when we go beyond ourselves and give ourselves to something more, to other men and women or to God.

We come to ourselves most often in prayer, for in prayer we go beyond our little self to the great selflessness, which is perhaps the best name for our true identity.

Identify yourself with God,

as Jesus did. Give your mind to God, your heart, your life to God, and you will find that God gives Himself through you: God's mind your mind, God's heart your heart, God's life your life.

You have powers you never knew you had. You are more than you have thought yourself to be. Believe!

A bird flies into a room. We open all the windows and try to edge it toward one. But often it continues to flutter blindly from corner to corner. Yet the windows are open. Nothing restrains it but itself. The whole sky beckons if it will but fly forth.

So we flutter about the little room in which we find ourselves, come to blind corners in our reasoning, beat vainly against the windowpanes that are our senses. Yet the windows of our faith are open upon infinity itself, if we will but fly forth.

When the littleness in us grows less, the greatness increases. When we are no longer bound to selfish ends, we are free.

When the separateness in us is dissolved, we are at one.

When we let go our limitations, we find ourselves beyond them.

Beyond them is God.

As beyond a wave there is the sea, and as the wave is not separate from the sea but extends back into the sea and shares the sea's strength, so beyond body, beyond mind, there is the selfless Self where each one of us knows that he is not separate and little and powerless but one with the Good Omnipotent itself. It is here that each of us knows, "I am the very best that is!"

As beyond a wave there is the sea, and as the wave is not separate from the sea but extends back into the sea and shares the sea's strength, so beyond body, beyond mind, there is the selfless Self where each one of us knows that he is not separate and little and powerless but one with the Good Omnipotent itself.

A Conversation With a Mayfly

One day as I sat thinking about the world and what it might mean, a mayfly blew against my window and clung there—delicate, translucent, trembling, frail—then rose, was caught by a passing breeze, and in a moment vanished.

This world, I thought, is vast and varied, crowded from endless end to endless end with countless marvels, all unaccountable, different, and strange. If this world has a Maker, whatever made it must be—whether Being or Principle—far above me, not only in power but in intelligence. And that being the case, it must also be far above me in love; for such an intelligence would not leave itself loveless.

But here is this mayfly, which lives only for a day, making winged love and fluttering on the summer breeze, and falls into a fish's mouth. Not even I, unloving as I am, would make a world where creatures are born to live a day, suffer and die. How can a world so cruel be the work of a love so intelligent as the Maker of this world would have to be?

How can this world have a Maker?

Then I cried out, "O God, if there is a God, explain this to me!"

I listened. Much to my surprise, I heard an answering voice. It was not God's. The mayfly had flown back and was clinging again to my windowpane. And this little creature was speaking.

"Because I will die," said the mayfly, "would you not let me be born?"

I would have been surprised to hear God speak; I was even more surprised to find myself in conversation with a mayfly. I could only mutter, "What is that you say?"

"I was saying," said the mayfly, "that it is true that I live only for a day, fluttering on the summer breeze and making winged love, and shortly fall into a fish's mouth. But because I will die, would you not let me be born?"

"Oh, that's not what I meant at all," I said.

"Then what did you mean?" said the mayfly.

"Why, I would have had you

born to be something much … I would have had you born to be …" Suddenly I was not sure just what I was going to say. "It's hard for me to say," I said. "But I would have made you different. Yes, wonderfully different!"

"I was afraid of that," said the mayfly.

"I wouldn't have made you such a delicate, frail creature, so easily destroyed. I'd have made you sturdy, strong, impervious to time and attack, able to survive for many years."

"And just how would you have accomplished that?" said the mayfly, fluttering its diaphanous wings. "Would you have made me,

say, like a big, clumsy beetle or perhaps like a fish even bigger and scalier than the fish you would protect me from? Or … no, I have it! Like a snapping turtle, with a heavy shell and a horny beak! They live a very long life, I hear. But I don't think I'd like that."

"Well, I certainly wouldn't have made you what you now are," I said. "I couldn't conceive of making something with such a little time to live—and even that little time so fraught with peril."

"Time? What is time?" said the mayfly. "Have you ever heard me complaining that I have too short a time?"

"I've never before even heard

"I was saying," said the mayfly, "that it is true that I live only for a day, fluttering on the summer breeze and making winged love, and shortly fall into a fish's mouth. But because I will die, would you not let me be born?"

you," I said.

"If you had," said the mayfly, "you would not have heard me talking about time. It is you who are always talking about time. And yes, complaining about it. You are always early or late. You have too little or too much. You are wistful about the past and apprehensive about the future. As for me, I do not creep like you from what has been to what will be. I only waft from now to now."

The mayfly fluttered into the air, letting the passing breeze waft him upward, wafted through a series of somersaults and gently wafted back against the window-pane. "Have you ever thought what it's like to be a mayfly?"

"As a matter of fact," I said, "It's because I was thinking of what it's like to be a mayfly that I got into this discussion. I was saying to myself that I couldn't see how, in a meaningful world, a creature could be made to live for a day and be gobbled up by a fish."

"Is that all you are capable of thinking of," said the mayfly, "how I live for a day and am gobbled up? That's like saying that to be a human being is to live for seventy years and then die in bed. I think that's a very small part of the affair.

"If you could feel what it's like to spread wings—and wings like gossamer!—and feel a sudden eddy of air ripple through your soul and lift you up, up, hardly more than air yourself—but what's the use! I should be smart enough to imagine what it might be like to be impalpable me."

I did not like being thought of as gross and unimaginative, but before I could think of a fitting reply, he rushed on. "You have a hard time even putting yourself in the experience of another human being, let alone another species. Oh, you observe what happens, but only as if it were happening to you. You observe, but you don't experience. You may take me apart, but you can't put me together, because you never look at me from the inside out, but only from the outside in. You never ask what it's like being a mayfly to a mayfly. You only ask what it's like to a human being."

"But your life is brief!" I said.

"To you—or to me?" said the mayfly. "And however that may be, I've never heard that life is to be measured by how long it lasts or by the way it ends."

"The fact remains, however, you have only a day. I can't believe there's anyone who wouldn't agree that's a pretty sorry lot."

"You say so," said the mayfly. "But let me ask again, when was it you heard us mayflies complain about our lot?"

The mayfly's attitude was beginning to annoy me. I thought to myself, This sorry little creature not only has a sad and short existence, it hasn't enough intelligence to complain about its sorry fate. Then I said aloud: "I was complaining for you. You may accept your fate, but I cannot. In fact, you make me doubt that there is any meaning in the world at all. I can't see how a God could create such a cruel and meaningless existence as a—as—"

"As a mayfly's?" finished the mayfly. "Cruel and meaningless to whom? Not to me, certainly. I find my existence very meaningful to me. And I have never heard of any commandment from God or any law of nature that decrees I must be meaningful to you.

"From what omniscient mountaintop, O man, do you decide that my dainty, amorous moment drifting on the summer wind has less meaning than your belabored, thought-tormented journey? With what measure, tell me, do you measure my misery or delight?"

"Forgive me, dear little mayfly," I said. "I'm not belittling may-

flies. I'm just using you mayflies to make my point. It's the world I'm questioning—and myself. For seeing you, I suddenly saw that we are, alas, all mayflies in a mayfly kind of world!"

"As to our all being mayflies," said the mayfly, "forgive me, dear little man, but I can think of nothing that so little resembles a mayfly as you."

"I just meant that in a general sense," I said. "I was trying to make the point that such a mayfly kind of world seems hard to explain in terms of a loving Maker."

"You aren't making general sense or any sense at all," said the mayfly. "It is only a world that is not a mayfly world which I find hard to explain in terms of a loving Maker."

"You don't understand what I'm trying to say, do you?" I said.

"You don't understand what you are trying to say, do you?" said the mayfly.

Now I had reached the end of my patience with this insect.

"You poor little mayfly," I said condescendingly. "As you have said, you are a mayfly and I am a man. 'Ah, the pity of it, the pity of it, imago!' " I was pleased with my twist on Shakespeare's line; in case you don't know, a mayfly is an imago.

"Shakespeare, isn't it?" said the mayfly. "From Othello, and badly out of context! 'Pity no more would be … were all as happy as we.' That's Blake, and much more appropriate to our discussion."

I was beginning to feel a little ridiculous debating the meaning of things with a mayfly, even one that read poetry, and it irritated me greatly to see him thinking he could outquote me.

"You poor little *ephemeroptera ephemeridae*, I do pity you!" I said.

"It is you who have named me that. But then, you call yourself Homo sapiens," said the mayfly, and I thought I heard it tittering under its antennae. "As to my proper name, it might surprise you to know that it is Sir Dalliance O'Day, Lord of the Eternal Moment, though some of my friends call me Lover Boy.

"You will never learn, I suppose, that your names are only your own way of looking at things, and no one else's. Certainly not a mayfly's—or God's. But enough of this. If I am an ephemerid, I am too ephemerally wise to waste my day in futile metaphysical argument.

"And I have a rendezvous. Her name is Lady Sans Souci, but I call her Saucy. That's more appropriate too."

The mayfly flew into the air, but a gust caught him and blew him hard against the wall. I cried out but quickly saw that he was unhurt.

"I say, old top, you are capable of pity! I'm glad to see that," said the mayfly, righting himself with a shimmer of flower-petal wings. "But think about that. Shall you be capable of pity, and that which made you not feel pity too? You can feel love—yes, even for someone as different as I; does that not say enough about your Maker?"

With a carefree dip and swoop, he went bobbing off out of sight, but before he vanished I caught the faint sound of his voice drifting back on the wind: "Because I will die, would you not let me be born?"

Then I heard a chorus of voices. I thought I could hear the voice of every living thing, of all that crawls and flies and swims and burrows, all that hunts and is hunted, all that pounces and is pounced upon; and all these voices cried as one: "Because we will die, would you not let us be born?"

Then I heard the mountains and rivers and oceans, and even the Earth and sun and all the stars, and they all cried as with one voice: "Because we will crumble and pass away, would you not let us have our mayfly moment drifting in the wind?"

Then I heard my own voice saying, "And you, because you will die, would you rather have not been born?"

I thought about this. I thought how I have sometimes wearied of life and sometimes been overwhelmed by pain and terror, and how at such times I may have cried out, "Would that I had never been!"

But I wondered if that is what I really wished. Not to suffer this moment, not to endure this pain, not to face this uncertainty—this I can wish. But to wish I had never been born—this I can wish only because I *have* been born. Because I have been, because I am, I may wish not to be. But had I never been?

To be, even for a moment! Besides this, is there anything that means so much, anything that even means? For the living may wish to die and what is may wish not to be, but what is not can have no wish; it cannot wish to be or not to be.

Then I had a vision of God, and I thought I heard God saying, "Go and be what is yours to be, mountain if you are mountain, human being if you are a human being, mayfly if you are mayfly." I saw all the infinite variety of things swarming forth—the things for the moment and the things for the millennia, the things known and the things unknown, the things imaginable and the things unimaginable. And I saw them all experiencing what is theirs to experience in order that they might be what they are.

I heard the Infinite Creative Force declaring: "Let there be!" I saw the Infinite Creative Force filling emptiness, forming the world, willing into being all the things that will to be, bringing forth out of the infinite nothing all the infinite somethings.

And I felt the Infinite Compassion embracing each thing as it went forth to be itself, each a unique, special, never-to-be-duplicated experience, with whatever experiences being what it was might call for.

Then I saw that a mayfly's being a mayfly demands certain risks and perils and anxieties and agonies. And, likewise, a mountain's being a mountain, and a human being's being a human being.

If the mayfly is to be a mayfly, it must suffer these risks and perils and anxieties and anguishes. But if to be what I am, I must be born just outside a hungry fish's mouth, will I not hope for a plenitude of fish? If I am a mayfly, will I not pray for a mayfly world? If I am a mayfly … ah, to be a mayfly! What else in all the world can be so meaningful, so desirable—if I am a mayfly!

I saw that each thing suffers and dies, but each has the unique experience of being itself, something exquisitely original and special, living a life nothing else has ever lived or ever will. And it is because each creature is the unique, original, and special thing it is that it has meaning. My meaning rises from the fact that I am not you, but I am myself.

Then I saw around me all the infinite host of living things, and I heard them singing, each one in a different voice, but all as with one thought:

"Thanks be to the Compassion so creative and the Creativity so compassionate that it has made it possible for me to be me, whatever that may be like and whatever that may call for."

And I lifted my voice in song and sang my praises too.

Then I heard a chorus of voices.
I thought I could hear the voice of every
living thing, of all that crawls and flies
and swims and burrows, all that hunts
and is hunted, all that pounces and is
pounced upon; and all these voices cried
as one: "Because we will die,
would you not let us be born?"
Then I heard the mountains and rivers
and oceans, and even the Earth and sun
and all the stars, and they all cried as with
one voice: "Because we will crumble and
pass away, would you not let us have our
mayfly moment drifting in the wind?"

XII.

Growth

God Sees That We Are Growing

We are all children, large or small,
some young, some older, that is all.
God, I am sure, does not expect
children to always be correct.
This Earth is but a little star
and we its human creatures are
not often brave or wise or strong
or true to what is best for long.
Yet through our clouds of dark unknowing,
I think God sees that we are growing;
God sees us stumble, sees us err,
but sees we are not what we were.
And when we turn from love and run
away from Truth, God does not shun
us then, but loves us all the more—
is this not what a God is for?
Children, you are the offspring of
our Mother Life, our Father Love.

215

The Hilltop Heart

If only you have a hilltop heart,
life's compass points lie far apart;
what heights and deeps life has, how far
the hilltop heart's horizons are!
Hills have a way of stretching minds;
lured-on imagination winds
up over crests and down through hollows.
Hills tug at the heart, and the heart follows,
dares the undared, tries the untried.
Hills always have another side;
if you make the climb up and descent,
you may find the valley of content.
Though a hilltop heart may never stand still,
yet the heart was meant for the top of a hill!

I've Come Up to Here

I believe I am making an immortal journey, and I've come up to here. That's all. I think that's all we need to say. I'm making an immortal journey. I've come up to here.

I love that phrase, "I've come up to here," because I think it describes the human condition. Here we are. Here and now is what we've come up to on this journey. I got the phrase from a Hopi Indian. It's a Hopi phrase. I got it in a way that utterly convinces me there's a lot more to the world than seems to be here.

I used to be responsible for teaching all Unity ministers, and I'd have special classes for them that weren't just religious; I believe ministers should know a lot about a lot of things. One time, in one of these classes, we were reading a biology book, *Man's Emerging Mind*, by a biologist named N. J. Berrill. It is a beautifully written book, full of stimulating ideas. In the middle of this book, he mentions the Hopi Indians, and he says in effect that in their language they have no way of putting an idea in the past or future. In English we do this by conjugating a verb. We put an "ed" on it and that puts it in the past, and we put a *shall* or *will* in front of it and that puts it in the future. When I read this I thought, "What would that do to you, if you had no tenses?" We are all prisoners of our language. You think the way you think to a great extent because you think in English and English has a certain structure, and if it had a different structure, the way you think would be different. If I had no way of making an easy past and easy future, what would that do to my thinking?

So I sent one of my students to the Kansas City Public Library to bring back what he could about the Hopis. Well, all he could find were a couple of books that showed little hogans on the mesas and a few Indians sitting in front of them. But, about two weeks later the tour guide at Unity Village called me on the phone and she said: "Jim, there's a couple down in the Silent Unity Visitors' Chapel who would like to meet you. Could you come down?" So I went down and she introduced me to Chief Frederick Whitebear of the Hopi Indians,

growth

and his wife Naomi.

What are the chances, just because you'd like to know something about the Hopis, of a Hopi chief walking into your office? It must be at least millions to one. You can say, "Oh, well, just a lucky coincidence." But I don't believe in lucky coincidences or unlucky ones, either.

As it turned out, Whitebear is probably the leading authority on the Hopis. He told me a number of things about them. Berrill, by the way, was not exactly right about their language. Among other things, Whitebear said, "Often when two Hopis meet, they will say to each other, 'Ah, so you've come up to here.'" I thought, "Isn't that a great phrase, because it's so true of us. It's a perfect description of the human condition. We've come up to here."

Chief Whitebear had come to see me because he'd had to come to a town in Kansas. An anthropologist was writing a book, *The Book of the Hopi*, and Chief Whitebear was his consultant. He's listed on the title page. It seems that he and his wife had liked my writing through the years, so they decided, "Let's go over to Unity Village and see if we can meet this man Freeman." So, in walked the Hopi chief. You may not believe this, but I believe that it was because I had sent out a call. And after meeting Whitebear and reading *The Book of the Hopi*, I can see if someone were going to respond to a mental call like mine, a Hopi Indian would be a likely responder. They are very unusual people with a long, long history of dedication and practice of spiritual principles. There is no question in my mind that Whitebear heard me and came.

218

One Step More

A hill is not too hard to climb
taken one step at a time.

One step is not too much to take;
one try is not too much to make.

One step, one try, one song, one smile
will shortly stretch into a mile.

And everything worthwhile was done
by small steps taken one by one.

To reach the goal you started for,
take one step more, take one step more!

One of My Most Vivid Memories

I have a grandson. One night, when he was three or four, I was carrying him in my arms. There was a huge full moon in the sky—oh, a glorious round moon—and I pointed it out to him and I kept saying, "Moon, Moon," and he'd look up at it and I'd say, "Moon, Moon." It was delightful. Then, about two or three weeks later, I was with him walking around in my backyard. It was afternoon, and suddenly he looked up and he pointed and said, "Look, Grandpa, Moon!" and I looked, and there was a day moon. Of course, I was delighted that he was smart enough to recognize that pale day moon as the Moon I'd pointed out to him. Then he held out his arms and said, "Give it to me, Grandpa." I thought, I wish I could. That's one of the most vivid memories I have. That moment in that yard, when he was reaching up for the Moon.

The Stone the Builders Rejected

Life does not demand, "Did you always do what you set out to do?" No one has ever done all he set out to do. No matter what we did, we thought we might do more. We might have run faster, thought higher, built the building more foursquare.

Did you hit the bull's-eye every time you fired? Why did you aim at such an easy target—and do you dare try one shot more?

Sometimes it is the distance we fell short that is the measure of our height.

We have all been given the same clay to work with. Some of us have been given a little more agile fingers, some a little more clay.

But it has never been those with the most clay who have made the most of it. Sometimes it has been those with the least clay; they had to stretch their minds.

Nor is it those with the most agile fingers. Sometimes it has been those with the least agile fingers. Sometimes it has only been after we have lost our fingers that we got down in earnest to what we had to do.

It is often the weakest lad who becomes the strongest man.

The stone the builders rejected has become the chief cornerstone.

A Handful of Earth

Do you think you are not much?

A handful of earth is not much. Yet if we knew how to draw forth the power contained in it, we could reshape the globe and everything on it.

If there is so much power in a handful of earth, how much power is in you, who are much more than a handful of earth.

If you could draw forth the power contained in you, you would change the history of the human race.

You may not be much, but you are enough.

One human is enough to change the world.

One human has changed the world many times—one human with a single thought, one human with a little faith, one human with a sense of something needing to be done that was his to do.

One human! You are one.

You probably had a better start in life than George Washington Carver, who was born a Negro slave. You probably had more education than Mahomet or Joan of Arc, who were illiterate, or Edison, whose teacher sent him home from school because he was a dunce, or even Shakespeare, who barely went through grammar school. You probably had better health than Epictetus, who was a cripple, or Homer, who was blind, or Beethoven, who was deaf when he wrote some of his best music, or Dostoevski, who was an epileptic.

You are probably younger than Grandma Moses, who was seventy-eight when she started to paint, and older than John Keats, who was dead when he was twenty-five.

Most of the things worth doing have been done by men and women who had no particular qualification for doing them.

They were just men and women who refused to settle for the obvious limitations.

Who placed on you the limitations you have settled for?

Who holds you back now?

Corn

Corn grows so fast you can hear it grow.
But the sound of growing things is no
sound for a careless heart to catch;
you need sharp ears and a heart to match,
a heart in tune with life, in love
with the world and all the wonder of
God's things! Then on a summer night
when everything inside is right
and everything outside is still
and your will is one with the one great will,
you lie and listen and you hear,
as much with the mind's as the body's ear,
shoot and blade and stalk unfold,
tassel and silk and ear of gold,
and you feel the urge, the urgency
of life, the welling will to be!
Then in the quietness you know
how passionately God's things grow;
you feel your spirit growing tall,
reaching to be one with all
reality! Heart's span by span
grows up the spiritual man!

Your Unknown World

We live in a time of reaching out. We send rockets into space to probe the Moon, Venus, Mars, the immensity beyond. We train giant telescopes on worlds so distant that measurement seems meaningless. We bring together our most brilliant minds, erect complex, ingenious machines, spend billions of dollars—even to begin the conquest.

What is out there? we ask, and dream what it will be like to journey into emptiness.

This is a noble project—to explore the world around us. Our minds shake the tree of the world, and the fruit of the knowledge of things has come dropping into our hands.

We are all dwellers in space; we make our habitation among stars and molecules. Out of their stuff we build our homes and even the bodies with which we build.

Our very word *real* comes from the ancient Latin word that means "a thing." So much are we a part of the world.

Yet, real as the world of things may seem, who thinks of themselves as a "thing"? There are times when we all feel more like observers of the world than a part of it. We view it, as it were, from somewhere else.

The outer world is all around us. We seem to live and move and have our being in it. It washes over us like a sea. Yet we sense that we ourselves are not of this sea but only voyagers through its deeps.

We are not children of the world but only dwellers in it. We are children of God.

If there is an outer world in which we dwell, there is also an inner world, at least as real, as vast in extent, as strange and rich and varied. It is not a world of space and time, of things and dimensions. It is a world of thought and feeling, of mind and spirit.

Here are deeps at least as deep as a sea. Here are heights at least as high as a mountain. Here are valleys; here are rivers; here are storms and calms, green pastures and still waters, dark nights and rosy dawns. We have in us a world.

And today, if we ask, "What is

If there is an outer world in which we dwell,
there is also an inner world,
at least as real, as vast in extent, as strange and
rich and varied. It is not a world of space and
time, of things and dimensions. It is a world
of thought and feeling, of mind and spirit.

out there?" We have begun to ask "What is in there?"

We have become aware that there is an unknown world within us.

It is a world about which we know very little. We have explored the Moon—and most of us have never explored ourselves.

We are full of desires, thoughts, feelings, powers, and potentialities that we are almost unaware of. Sometimes we seem to live like a water skipper on the surface of a deep well. But we are not merely a skipper on the surface; we are the well and all that it contains, its creatures and its deeps, at the source one with all the waters of the world.

Have you ever thought how little you know about you?

What is the world within you like? Where is it? When you turn within, where do you turn? Is it to some center in your body? or in your head?

Has it ever occurred to you that your inner world is not a place? It is not inside your body or your head. Your inner world is not "a-whereness"; it is awareness.

Pick up a book, observe its covers, turn its pages, note the black lines of type on the white sheets of paper. Is this the book?

It is the outward form of the book, but there is infinitely more to a book than this. A book exists more in the inner world than in the outer world. A book is not so much an object in space as it is an idea in mind. Every copy of it can be burned, yet that book will remain as alive as ever—as long as we hold it in mind.

If this is true of a book, is it not much more true of a human being? His physical appearance is among the least important things about him—and becomes even less important the better we get to know him. After a time we may scarcely be aware of it; people who are close to us change appearance, and we do not even see the change.

It is what you are within that is important. People, like books, may sometimes have lovely covers and yet have little substance inside. And great books and people often come to our hand dog-eared, plain, and worn. But the truth and the beauty shine from within.

So it is with you.

Within you are your true treasures—treasures yet untouched. Here are mines of mind richer than Golconda, resources of Spirit beside which the wealth of the Indies is paltry. The discoveries that we have made, the powers that we have tapped—these are small beside the powers within that lie waiting to be tapped, the discoveries within that lie waiting to be made.

In us, for instance, is a power to heal. It is at work all the time. Most of the time we are unaware of it; it is quietly repairing cells, carrying off wastes, nourishing tissues, and healing wounds. But occasionally it reveals itself in one of us in some remarkable way. A man

is mortally ill; and suddenly, with no explanation, the growth vanishes, the wound heals, the heart restores itself. If there has been prayer—if, say, the man has gone to Lourdes or written to Silent Unity—we exclaim, "A miracle!" If not, we just wonder and rejoice.

But the fact is that this inner power of healing, of life, is not an extraordinary power. It is in all of us all the time. It is a natural part of our inner world. But we have not yet learned how to make it work through us.

Constantly, twenty-four hours a day, part of us is supervising all the fantastically complicated operations of our bodies. Effortlessly, in a single cell, the superscientist in us performs functions that the world's most learned chemists cannot duplicate in acres of factories.

And these are only a fraction of the powers the mind-giant in us possesses.

There are people who in a moment do mathematical feats of unbelievable difficulty. Almost as fast as anyone can present a problem, they give the answer.

There are others who have equally remarkable powers of memory. They have only to glance at a page once to have it fixed in mind for years.

In our time we are beginning to explore yet other powers. Experimenters in the field of parapsychology are discovering that we have powers we have not even dreamed of.

Space does not exist in the world within us; we are anywhere with the speed of thought. Time does not exist; we are in the past or future as easily as in the present. Now we go only in imagination—but the power is there—and we shall learn to use it, not merely to imagine but actually to experience.

Is there one of us who does not have a sense of a world within at least as vast and strange as the world outside? Is there one of us who has not now and then touched powers beyond his common ones?

Sometimes we catch only a momentary flash of something not quite understood. But sometimes we see something happen that makes us suddenly aware that there is a power within beside which the power in the atom, the power that holds the stars in their courses, is puny.

A Moses needs to part a Red Sea. The Mormons need to stem an invasion of crickets. A George Müller needs to feed the hungry boys in his orphanage at Bristol, England. An Eddie Rickenbacker needs to feed the men afloat with him in a rubber life raft.

Our greatest triumphs are all triumphs of mind. Someone lays hold on an idea in mind and finds—oh, ever-recurring miracle!—that she has grasped the world of things outside her and changed it nearer to her heart's desire.

A man named Henry Ford was born more than a hundred years ago, the son of a farmer. He changed the habits of his nation. What with? With the intuitive power within him.

A man named Mohammed, an illiterate caravan guide, changed a few tribes of desert nomads into a force that conquered much of the Earth, founded a great culture, and established a religion that is still influencing more than four hundred million people. Where did he find such a capacity? One night in a cave, communing alone, he had a revelation from within.

A fourteen-year-old girl named Joan, the illiterate daughter of a poor peasant in a remote part of France, heard voices telling her to go to her king and lead his army to free her country from the enemies that had seized most of it. She did it! Where did she hear the voices? Within.

A man named Shakespeare, with only a grammar-school education, wrote the most beautiful English and the greatest plays ever written. Where did the words come from? From within him.

A man named Mozart began to compose music when he was five years old, and he wrote so many unsurpassed pieces that it takes a catalog just to list the titles. Where did this music flow from? From within.

A man named Edison, deaf and with only three months in public school, was responsible for so many inventions that our whole way of life has been changed by them—I write this sentence by the light of one. What did he draw on? The world within him.

A man named Jesus, a carpenter's son, living in an obscure village in an obscure province that he never left, changed every one of us. Where did the power come from to bring about this change? He told us. "The Father who dwells in me, does his works," he said (Jn. 14:10). And he said further to each one of us, "God is within you" (Lk. 17:21 KJV).

These are geniuses, prophets, saviours, we say. But the greatest of them promised that we could do even greater things than he did.

These men and women did not touch a power that only they had. They touched a power that all of us have.

In us is a creative spirit. We touch it occasionally, and out of the unknown, like sparks from a cosmic fire, come revelations of truth, visions of beauty, fresh forms of life and joy. Not out of a cloud nor out of the hand of a Zeus the lightning flashes, but out of ourselves. In us are the everlasting springs of life. In us is the secret place of the Most High.

Remember the story of the king's son who was taken from his father at birth and brought up in a woodchopper's hut, believing he was a woodchopper?

Why are we living like woodchoppers? We are—all of us—a king's sons and daughters.

What are we doing in this hut of husks? We are the children of Mind, made in the image of a divine idea. We have a kingdom that is ours for the claiming—the kingdom of consciousness, the inner country of the heart and mind, the world of ideas.

Is there a chart that we can follow as we make this unknown world our own? Is there a map of

In us is a creative spirit.
We touch it occasionally, and out of the unknown, like sparks from a cosmic fire, come revelations of truth, visions of beauty, fresh forms of life and joy. Not out of a cloud nor out of the hand of a Zeus the lightning flashes, but out of ourselves. In us are the everlasting springs of life.

mind, an atlas of the heart?

Some who have gone before us have left records of their explorations. Cartographers of Spirit, they tell us how we may begin our voyage.

"Be still, and know," (Ps. 46: 10) they say and lay down disciplines of thought and feeling and desire.

"Go into your room and shut the door and pray to your Father who is in secret" (Mt. 6:6). This the Way-Shower told us. "Follow me," (Mt. 19:21) he said. "Seek, and ye shall find" (Mt. 7:7 KJV).

But we have scarcely made a landing on this shore. Before us lies a hemisphere of being.

Is there infinity outside? Do not think that there is less than infinity inside. In is just like out—it is without boundaries. You have a world within you infinite in extent

and in potentiality, an unknown world where you must make the quest and conquest of yourself.

How high can you go? As high as you can hope.

How deep can you go? As deep as you can feel.

How far can you go? As far as you can imagine.

Go as far as thought will take you, and when you have come to the perfection of Truth, you will have found beauty of Spirit.

Go as far as Spirit will take you, and when you have come to the perfection of beauty, you will have found a heart of love.

Go as far as love will take you, and when you have come to the perfection of love, you will have found the fulfillment of desire.

The fulfillment of desire is God.

To Soar

A will in me
won't settle for
less than the more
I ought to be.

I feel it strain
against the tug
of the tether, hug
of the downward rein.

Each particle
throughout my whole
being, body and soul,
feels the mystic pull

To be more than I
have dreamed I might
be, child of light
and the Most High.

Although the Crowd

Although the crowd stood up to cheer
the leap by which you cleared the bar,
the leap by which you failed to clear
may measure what you truly are.

At fortune's lowest ebb a man
may be the closest to the crest;
the race in which he also ran
may be the one he ran the best.

Aim

The runner who has always won
and never staggered to defeat
has only half-learned how to run;
his victory is incomplete
who never knew the dust and shame
of failure, straining in the dark!
He only had too low an aim
who has not ever missed the mark.

Of Freedom and Fences

Now let us take a look at freedom. Freedom! The word rings like a bell, doesn't it? It lifts the heart and stirs the passions. But just what is freedom? How free is free? How free can I be? How free can anyone be?

I have a dog, a saluki, a large, beautiful, extremely active dog. I live in a house with a large yard, almost a couple of acres. My dog has free access to the yard at all times through her own swinging door, and in house and yard she lives a very free life, for the most part doing only what she wants to do. My wife and I make few demands on her, probably fewer than she makes on us. She flies from one end of the yard to the other, chasing anything that happens to be going by on the street or any squirrel, cat, rabbit, or bird that ventures into the yard that she takes it into her head to chase.

My yard is fenced, but much of it is not a high fence, mainly ornamental. The fence is more a mental limit than a physical obstacle. Any time she wished, she could be over it like the wind and off across the city. Not the fence, but only her own acceptance of the fence keeps her in the yard.

My dog and her fence have made me think about freedom in very different terms than I had ever thought about it before. I have come to realize that the fence does not keep her in bondage; it keeps her free!

Suppose she did jump the fence and go wandering off? Would she be free? Freer than she now is? Out in the streets is a world of laws against unleashed dogs, angry neighbors, unfriendly dogs, dogcatchers, and speeding cars. How free would she be skittering frightened and bewildered through the unfamiliar maze of the city's streets? Have you ever seen a lost dog?

In the world that lies beyond the fence, there is no way she could remain free for long; at best, she would be taken into the house of some kind person; at worst, she would be locked up in the dog pound or even run over. The fence does not limit her freedom as much as it guarantees it. It does not keep

233

My yard is fenced, but much of it is not a high fence, mainly ornamental. The fence is more a mental limit than a physical obstacle. Any time she wished, she could be over it like the wind and off across the city. Not the fence, but only her own acceptance of the fence keeps her in the yard. My dog and her fence have made me think about freedom in very different terms than I had ever thought about it before. I have come to realize that the fence does not keep her in bondage; **it keeps her free!**

her freedom from her. On the contrary, it marks how far she can go and not lose her freedom—relative freedom, it is true, but which of us has any other kind?

What limits my dog's freedom is not that fence but the fact that she is a saluki who has to live in Lee's Summit, Missouri, United States of America, on the continent of North America and the planet Earth. Similar limitations determine the freedom of us all.

Freedom is and always must be a relative matter. If I am wise, I do not insist on flying just because I would like to have wings. I walk when I have to. I may be free to step out of a window, but the moment I do, I lose my freedom. I lose it emphatically; I am made captive and plummeted to Earth by forces over which I have no control. I have asserted my freedom beyond my power to maintain it. I have gone beyond my fence.

I built my dog's fence. In the case of human beings, they themselves may have to build their fences. Not all, of course. Many of our fences have been built by wise and loving people who lived before us, examined the world—as I have for my dog—and realized where fences were needed if they were to preserve, and not lose, their liberty. If we are wise, we accept the fences raised for us by laws, by tradition, by religious belief, by the moral code, by good manners and consideration.

For if we go too far beyond the fences of reasonable restraint, we may find we have not extended our freedom, we have lost what freedom we had. To go too far is to come up short.

I wonder if we as a nation are still here after two hundred years because the founding fathers were as aware of fences as they were of freedom when they wrote the Declaration of Independence. For they set up a very fenced-in freedom, but it was one within which they could unite to get the country started and within which we have been able—in spite of all the persisting inequities—to be the freest people the human race has so far managed to produce.

In our time many people insist on acting as if there are no fences. "I must be free!" they assert, and they think this means they have the right to act, say, or think as they please.

You have only to think about it to see that if everyone were free to do whatever he or she wished to do, it would result not in freedom but in chaos. The world would become a hodgepodge, impossible work of infinite whim.

We are created to be free. The newborn child becomes enraged if you pinion her, and we never happily submit to domination, even our own. We are not puppets, no, not even God's! God made us to be free, for He made us in His image. That is why in the heart of every person stirs the desire freely to express his God-potential. That is why we feel a discontent with anything less than freedom. But we misinterpret it when we feel that it tells us to throw off every restraint, every limitation.

There are two kinds of freedom

I wonder if we as a nation are still here after two hundred years because the founding fathers were as aware of fences as they were of freedom when they wrote the Declaration of Independence. For they set up a very fenced-in freedom, but it was one within which they could unite to get the country started and within which we have been able—in spite of all the persisting inequities—to be the freest people the human race has so far managed to produce.

in the world. We have to be free *from* and free *to*. But sometimes we try to be free *from* what we should be free *to*, and free *to* what we should be free *from*. Then, in the name of freedom, we enslave ourselves.

For to be free means to be free *from* everything that keeps us from achieving our maximum potential, everything that weakens us, everything that tends to make us less than the most we are capable of being. And it means to be free *to* grow, to achieve dominion over our self and all the forces at work in us, to develop and express our creative powers.

The freedom that is God's free child's is not an easy freedom. It comes only with growth. It comes only with strength. It comes only with the power to stand firm and persevere. It comes only with mastery. And mastery comes only out of discipline.

Without discipline there is no freedom. My dog has helped me to learn this too. For us to enjoy a free walk together on a country afternoon, she must have learned to heel, come, and stay when I tell her to. When she was a puppy, we both went to obedience school, and there I learned that if I were to become the master, I had first to

master myself. Getting her to obey was not hard once I had learned to obey. Her discipline depended almost entirely on how disciplined I was. We are, all of us, freest when we have the maximum control over ourselves and our lives, when we can say to ourselves, "Go!" and we may go, and when we can say, "Stay!" and we stay.

The undisciplined life, the unrestrained life, is not the freest life; it is the least free. The undisciplined are imprisoned by their own lack of strength and skill. Instead of mounting on their limitations and learning to ride them to triumph, they let their limitations ride them.

The skater flying across the ice, how effortlessly she weaves through with fantastic patterns! The musician improvising at the piano, how freely her spirit ranges over the keys, fountains of music cascading from her fingertips! The basketball player, how carelessly he flicks the ball over his shoulder that it should fall so cleanly through the net! And the football player, with what unpremeditated art he spins through the field of tacklers intent on stopping him.

How free! How beautiful! we exclaim. But we know that this beautiful freedom can come only

Without discipline there is no freedom.

My dog has helped me to learn this too. For us to enjoy a free walk together on a country afternoon, she must have learned to heel, come, and stay when I tell her to. When she was a puppy, we both went to obedience school, and there I learned that if I were to become the master, I had first to master myself. Getting her to obey was not hard once I had learned to obey. Her discipline depended almost entirely on how disciplined I was. We are, all of us, freest when we have the maximum control over ourselves and our lives, when we can say to ourselves, "Go!" and we may go, and when we can say, "Stay!" and we stay.

after many months, many years of the hardest, most persistent practice. The power to be free had to be first of all the will to submit.

Where there are no fences, there is no freedom—not for long. Sometimes I think no one must know the meaning or the value of freedom better than the men and women in Alcoholics Anonymous. They have met their challenge and made it their conquest. They have taken the measure of their limitations and made it the measure of their freedom. They have learned how to live freely—within their fences. The peaks of freedom never have been scaled except by those who had the courage and the will to submit to the necessities of the endeavor.

"Where the Spirit of the Lord is, there is liberty." And the Spirit of the Lord is wisdom, strength, self-control. Even more, it is control by the highest forces and highest elements in our being.

XIII.
Christmas

If Every Day Were Christmas

If every day were Christmas,
how different life would be,
if not one day but all the year
were ruled by charity.
Had we the faith in miracles
a child has Christmas morn,
each day would be love's manger
and Christ would be reborn
in us again to change and heal
our outworn wars and ways—
had we a child's or shepherd's gift
for wonderment and praise!
Yet every day is Christmas
when we have learned to live
by love's law, learned not how to get
but only how to give;
and like a child can wonder
and like a child can pray,
but have the grown-up wisdom
to give ourselves away.

239

Christmas:
A Celebration of Imagination

From my earliest memory I have been in love with Christmas and, as with everything one loves, a little fearful about it, fearful that it may disappoint me, fearful that somehow sometime it will not be there when I look.

No other day of the year has such power to stir and excite us—though Christmas is not just a day, it is a season. The year does not have four seasons; it has a fifth: Christmas. And Christmas is at least as long as the other four. I have seen springs that hardly lasted a week and falls that weren't much longer, while Christmas for most people begins no later than Thanksgiving Day, when the lights go on in shopping centers, and lasts till Twelfth Night when we make a bonfire of the trees.

When you are a small boy, you are never unaware of Christmas, for you have been warned that Santa Claus or God or somebody is keeping a strict account of your misbehavior, and what you are going to get for Christmas depends on how bad you weren't. I was always threatened with coal—or perhaps it was switches—in my stocking. And since I knew I had been bad, I always got out of bed on Christmas morning with a great deal of anxiety. However, the stocking was always plumped with goodies.

Also, every year my parents debated whether or not they should have a tree. Probably the debate was meant to keep me on tenterhooks. If so, it succeeded. For I was never sure until I saw it in the parlor, resplendent with tinsel and baubles, that a tree would be there.

Also, though I kept up the pretense as long as I could, I think I knew from my earliest years that there really was no Santa, and so there really was the possibility that there wouldn't be a Christmas. That's a frightening thought for most of us children, isn't it?

What with all my fevers of expectation, deliriums of imagination, and fits of fear, I was usually

240

The year does not have four seasons; it has a fifth: Christmas. And Christmas is at least as long as the other four. I have seen springs that hardly lasted a week and falls that weren't much longer, while Christmas for most people begins no later than Thanksgiving Day, when the lights go on in shopping centers, and lasts till Twelfth Night when we make a bonfire of the trees.

Christmas

sick by Christmas, with an upset stomach and a runny nose. I am glad to say that the holiday no longer affects me so disastrously.

If some of you who read my writing have thought that I have always been a perfect model of spiritual composure, alas, you know now that it has taken me years of prayer just to calm down Christmas. Maybe that's because at heart I am still a very small boy (if you ask my wife she will tell you there is no doubt about that); one would have to be to write poetry—or Christmas fables!—in a world that seems to have sold its soul to its advertisers and expects to be saved by science.

I have worked at Unity School of Christianity almost all my adult life. And Unity School publishes magazines, and those magazines always have a December issue. I don't believe anybody in the publishing business has ever put out a December magazine without Christmas in it.

So editors here have always been delighted that they had this Christmas-crazed boy handy. All they had to do was wave a picture of a candle or a fir tree or almost anything Christmasy in front of him and whisper, "It's Christmas, Jim, can you write something?"

and very shortly out would come at least a short piece of Christmas verse.

For more than forty years I do not believe there has been a Christmas when I have not written at least one piece, prose or verse—and usually several pieces—about Christmas. Do not get the idea I have written just on demand. I have written because I love Christmas—and Unity! I have written dozens of Christmas things that have never been published; I wrote them because I wanted to write them; some thought or incident sparked my inspiration and I wrote.

However, it is only recently that I have written stories. For one thing, Unity periodicals did not seem to me to invite stories, and also, I liked writing poetry—or prose that was like poetry.

Telling you how I write and how I happened to start writing these stories—as well as I can remember—may give you a little insight into the curious and unforeseeable way in which the creative process works.

I remember clearly how I wrote the first fable. I had been asked to read some of my Christmas poetry to a business women's group in Lee's Summit. The meeting was on a Sunday afternoon in a church. After I read my poems, I was anxious to get away as soon as I could, because the Chiefs—Kansas City's football team—were playing an out-of-town game and I wanted to watch them on television. I can't remember whether they won or lost the game, for as I watched it, my thought kept drifting back to Christmas. I fell to thinking about the birth of Jesus and how it took place—in a stable, of all places! I have always loved that. I got to thinking about the animals in the stable. There is a legend that when Jesus was born, the animals that were present at his birth were given the power of speech so that they could praise him; and ever since on Christmas Eve at midnight the animals in the barnyard can speak. As I thought about the legend, this poem began to form itself in my mind:

At Christmas a spell is said to steal
at midnight over all dumb things
so that any of them that would can kneel
for a moment under angel wings.

And an angel song will fill their throats

till they sing as none before have sung.
Lord, when You teach dumb things their notes,
will You not touch my stumbling tongue?

For I, Your human creature, come
on a night when there is no star to see,
and kneel and wait like all things dumb
for the angel song to be sung in me.

After I had written the poem, I continued to think about the animals. I wondered which ones had been there, and I began to count them off: donkey, ox, sheep, goat, these certainly—perhaps some chickens and geese, and surely a mouse or two, and a few birds flying in the loft. Suddenly I thought: Whatever animals might have been there, there is one that could not have been present—the pig! Jesus' family was Jewish.

Immediately my heart went out to the little pig that could not have been there, and in a matter of minutes I was writing "The Tale of a Pig."

Oh, I don't mean it was written in minutes. As I recall, it took weeks. I lavished every skill I had

Christmas

on it. Writing it was a labor of love.

But once I had it written, I did not know what to do with it. I have never been much at marketing. I have no agent, and they are indispensable if you are going to sell what you write. Agents don't care for poets; they bolt the door and lock the windows when they hear that one is in the neighborhood.

Once I talked to my editor at Doubleday about printing my poetry; he shuddered, bared his teeth, and hissed: "You can't sell the stuff. We print fifteen hundred volumes and palm off a thousand of them on bookstores. With luck they sell maybe five hundred and send the other five hundred back to us." I also talked to him once about my Christmas stories. He shuddered in the same way, made the sign of the cross, and backed out of the room.

But I had enjoyed writing the story—oh, I truly had! If you have never written something that is pure imagination, you can't know the sheer delight of concentrating as intensely as you can on something that is and isn't at the same time, letting your mind soar to catch ideas you did not even know were there until you caught them,

excitedly pouring out and dubiously stumbling over words, and slowly seeing something formless find a form, something that was not there until you put it down, something so elusively illusion that sometimes you, the author, do not know what it is going to be until you have written and rewritten it and have the final words on paper and have read it.

I enjoyed writing the story so much that I wrote a second one, this time about an "Angel With a Broken Wing."

I am not sure from what obscure source the idea for it first filtered through. Perhaps it was from a joke about an angel with a broken wing one of my students had told me years before the thought occurred to me to write a story about such an angel. The joke had nothing to do with the story, but I had never forgotten it. I make speeches on religious subjects, and there seem to be very few religious jokes. At least I have heard only a few. So any I hear are never forgotten, not if there is even a remote hope they can be repeated in church; most of them can't.

Jokes are an absolute necessity for any speaker who hopes to keep his audience awake without having the ushers walk up and down the aisles with a padded pole and thump anyone they see nodding (a device New England preachers used two hundred years ago). When I decided to become a speaker, my first act was to buy a joke book.

Laughter, I have felt, should be held almost as holy as prayers. God, I am certain, has a sense of humor. He would have to have. To make people smile—surely this must be one of the most sacred acts a human being can perform.

But as I said, the joke had nothing to do with the story except that it planted an angel with a broken wing in my mind. My mind was already full of angels.

I have always loved the thought of angels. Unbelievable as it may seem to you—most of the time it seems unbelievable to me—I believe in them.

Most of my Unity friends say that angels are winged thoughts. Zarathustra, who almost invented angels, named his chief archangel Vohu Manah, Good Thought. And I won't argue that this is what angels are. But who shall say what forms thoughts may assume? Anything from gods to galaxies, no? But the question then becomes, Are the gods and galaxies thoughts or are the thoughts gods and galaxies?

I won't say what angels look like, but oh, I can tell you how they feel. They feel reassuring.

I know this makes me hopelessly out of touch with the times, but I would rather be medieval and look for angels, winged and singing, than be modern and look for little green men in a flying saucer from Mars.

I even think I have known a few angels. They looked just like us, and they never told me they were angels; perhaps they did not know. It may be that when an angel takes human form, one of the conditions is that the angel will not remember what he or she was before, just as we don't remember if we have lived before.

It would not surprise me at all to find I have a guardian angel. God knows I have needed one! At a number of critical times in my life, I have been protected against myself and my own stupid desires and have made decisions wiser than I intended to make. I often feel angels very close. Sometimes this has been embarrassing. I hope they are polite enough to know that on occasion they need to depart on some heavenly errand or at least turn away, shut their eyes, and pray. But then I am sure they expect me to be human as I expect them to be angelic.

I am always looking for them—or not so much looking as listening. I think when God has something to say God sends an angel. Many times I wake at two or three o'clock in the morning, and lying there in bed, I say, "God, have You anything to say? If You do, I'll be glad to get up and write it down." Then I lie there and listen. And it has been amazing how often when I listen, I hear. It's hard on sleep but wonderful for the inspiration. As a matter of fact, I got up at three o'clock this morning, and it's four as I write this.

Since I've always had this warm feeling about angels, it was natural that I should write about them, especially when I wanted to write about Christmas. Angels and Christmas have much in common—or should I say, uncommon? They go together like April and rain, May and flowers, June and weddings.

Naming the angel did not occur until I was writing the story, and of course the moment he told me his name the story took a different course.

The boy in the story, Johnnie, and his brothers were real children. I was at their home one win-

try day, and the football game in the snow, with Johnnie in his bare feet and his brothers pummeling him, actually took place. Perhaps as I heard the father exasperatedly tell me that Johnnie just wasn't like his brothers, the story began to take form.

You can see from this what unrelated incidents—a joke about an angel, some brothers playing football in the snow—somehow are brought together in the mind to make a story. I guess it's a lot like the way a cook creates a dish. The cook may throw into the pot anything from a rabbit to a radish and a touch of nutmeg, but when these are stirred together, out comes, not separate ingredients, but a single succulent delight.

I wrote these first two stories, "The Tale of a Pig" and "Angel With a Broken Wing," just for the joy of writing them. I had no idea where or whether they might be published. It did not occur to me that Unity would consider printing them; they never published fiction, and certainly no fiction like mine. My Doubleday editor told me once: "Our salesmen have a hard time selling your books. They can't tell the bookseller what shelf to put them on—whether they're religion or fairy tales, prose or poetry, for children or adults." I understand how he felt; I'm not sure myself.

But it happened that the editor of *Unity Magazine* was fond of my writing. I often shared some of my writing with him that I knew he would not print in *Unity Magazine*. One day I happened to tell him about these Christmas stories. He said he would like to read them, so I let him have them. Much to my surprise, he told me, "Jim, I'm going to keep 'The Tale of a Pig' and print it next Christmas in *Unity Magazine*."

But the editor was required to temporarily leave the magazine. His assistants did not want to print the story—*Unity Magazine* had never carried anything like this! Still, they felt they had to. So they buried it back in the magazine and cut it up on every page with blue-lined boxes containing profound quotations from Emerson and Kierkegaard—that way the page was not entirely wasted; it had a foolish fable on it, but also it had some serious thoughts.

However, a lot of readers liked the story; more wrote to the editor about the story than about anything else in the magazine. This surprised his assistants. It did not surprise me, even though, as I say,

I have always loved the thought of angels. Unbelievable as it may seem to you—most of the time it seems unbelievable to me—I believe in them. Most of my Unity friends say that angels are winged thoughts. Zarathustra, who almost invented angels, named his chief archangel Vohu Manah, Good Thought. And I won't argue that this is what angels are. But who shall say what forms thoughts may assume? Anything from gods to galaxies, no? But the question then becomes, **Are the gods and galaxies thoughts or are the thoughts gods and galaxies?**

Christmas

I, too, had wondered if the story belonged in *Unity Magazine*. I expect people to like what I write. I get a kick out of writing it, so I think you'll get a kick out of reading it. I am capable of smiling or weeping when I read what I have written, just as I hope you are.

It surprises me when people write and say they don't like what I have written; I am sorry to say this occasionally happens; some have even canceled their subscriptions.

Writing is an emotional task for me. I write—and rewrite—with a lead pencil. Words and phrases come gushing or dribbling out, some sparkling, some dull, some instantly recognized as right, some struck through almost as they are written down. My writing may be so marked through and written over that sometimes when I finally start to type it, I can hardly decipher the words or string the sentences together in a sensible order.

I do not outline, so I am not sure where I am going until I get there. Some of you with especially logical minds may be declaring, "Oh, how I wish he would!" But as I have said, I depend on my angels to be my guides—remember, they have wings!—and so at times I may find myself touching some thought far above my reach.

I don't mean that I abandon logic. Clarity is a passion with me. Few writers this side of comic books use shorter words or simpler sentences, though there is a hundred-word sentence in this piece that may make you question this. I try to write so that you can interpret what I have written without having to run to a dictionary or a grammar book. I want to make my meaning clear.

But meaning is not enough. I want my meaning to sound like a music, and not only to speak clearly to your mind but to sing exultingly in your heart.

Anyway, when a lot of people told *Unity Magazine*'s editor they liked "The Tale of a Pig," he told me he was going to print "Angel With a Broken Wing" too. I asked him if he wanted me to send him the manuscript, but he said that I wouldn't have to. He had made a copy when he had it, as he was sure the stories would be popular.

So the next Christmas he printed "Angel With a Broken Wing." Then he said to me: "Now your Christmas story is a Unity tradition. Our readers will look for them. I expect you to give me a Christmas story each year."

And so I have—ten of them—

and they have been collected in a wondrous book called *Once Upon a Christmas*.

People often ask me which of my stories I like best. I suppose I have my favorites, but even if I were sure, I wouldn't tell.

My mind is constantly sweeping the visible and invisible ethers; I am never without a pad and pencil—I won't buy a shirt that has no pockets—and now I also carry a small recorder. I put down any lines and phrases that happen my way on slips of paper that I squirrel away in manila folders. Especially when I have an assignment and the hour to deliver draws near and nothing has yet come, my mind races back and forth in a fluster of anxiety and expectation, probing into every unlikely corner, turning over any unlikely stones—sermons have been found in them, it has been observed—and above all looking hopefully to God—or at least, my angels. I have had ideas come singing into my head from the most unlikely sources and at impossible times. It is a very happy experience to have something start to write itself in your head at four o'clock in the morning when at eight o'clock you have to deliver a finished piece of writing.

As I have said, I love Christ-mas. Many people rail at it as too commercial. And it is commercial. Christmas is as worldly as it is holy; it mixes the secular and the religious so that we cannot tell them apart. But isn't that the way we would like things to be? Wouldn't it be a better world if things were like that all year long? If every day had something of religion in it, and religion had something of every day? If we took the gaily wrapped gifts, the cards, the decorations in the stores and streets, Christmas trees, and Santa out of Christmas, as some people would like to do, it would no longer be Christmas. It might be wholly holy, but it would also be very dull.

There are even those who would take the wonder out of the wondertale itself, if they could. They dissect the language of the Bible to show that the writers did not really mean to say that Mary was a virgin; she was merely a maiden. And every year a scientist or two proves that the Star was not an unexplainable glow in the sky, but a conjunction of planets, or a nova recorded by Chinese astronomers, or something equally dull and reasonable.

I say leave Christmas alone. Christmas is a wonder and a mag-

Christmas

ic, meant to cheer the heart, not argue with the mind. And that is what it ought to be.

So you eat too much, drink too much, spend too much—and afterward wish you hadn't. Perhaps on occasion the human spirit needs to burst beyond its decorous and sensible bounds, and what better moment can it pick than this, when winter days are at their shortest and grayest and the nights are chilly and long. (My apologies to Australia, but perhaps there is no less need of such a gala moment when the humid heat of summer seeps across our souls. For hundreds of years Midsummer's Eve was a celebration almost as festive as Christmas, and why do you think we enjoy Fourth of July fireworks and picnics in the park?)

Christmas sends Santa—the glorious grandfather of us all—out across the empty skies to bring gifts to every child in the world. There has to be something more than self-concern in the human heart to make us dream up such a warm and selfless old fellow! There he stands before us—on street corners, in shopping centers, in stores—and we have at least to stop and consider, no matter how miserly we may be, the holy duty and the human joy of giving!

Christmas is a time of feasting, and if we can, we feast; but also Christmas makes us aware that there are hungry and shelterless and lonely people in the world. It prompts us to reach at least into our pockets, if not into our hearts, to share our feast with them.

Christmas brings the green tree into our house—yes, even if today it is pink and artificial—and loads it with ornaments.

Christmas is as worldly as it is holy; it mixes the secular and the religious so that we cannot tell them apart. But isn't that the way we would like things to be? Wouldn't it be a better world if things were like that all year long? If every day had something of religion in it, and religion had something of every day?

250

To come downstairs when you are three and see in the corner, which the night before had been bare, a Christmas tree laden with baubles and glowing with lights—will life ever offer a more magic moment?

Christmas makes us add a touch of color to our everyday rooms and everyday life and puts a bright wreath or at least a green sprig on our front door as if we would say to all the world that there live in this house warm people who delight in beauty and believe in joy and want to share a little of it with you and that you would be welcome if you should come in.

Christmas makes us turn from our electric incandescence back to candles. Candles cast a very small light, but it is a light by which we may see one another's inner worth and beauty. Though it cannot warm our hands, it warms our hearts.

And even the jostling hurly-burly of the shopping centers— oh, I am sure we can thank our commercial instincts for them, but who is so dull of soul that he would not like to make at least one Christmas trip to one of them. For we go not only to buy, but also to satisfy our deep desire to rub elbows and spirits with our fellows, to press close and be pressed close into the bosom of humankind.

The festival of wonder, Christmas above all celebrates imagination.

For this is the kingdom and the power and the glory of imagination. It does not depend on the things we have, costly and beautiful and various though these may be; the things we have depend on it.

Perhaps some such Christmas as is described in the story is at least one of the reasons I write about Christmas.

And that is what I hope Christmas will always be, the celebration of imagination, with its power to warm our heart on a snowy day and sprinkle glitter on a dark one, to give us the goodwill to wish a merry Christmas though there is not much to feel merry about, to give us the faith to believe that life is not humdrum existence, but is capable of unbelievable wonder, and in the stable that is the human heart, to know God Himself may make His appearance.

And that is what I hope Christmas will always be, **the celebration of imagination,** with its power to warm our heart on a snowy day and sprinkle glitter on a dark one, to give us the goodwill to wish a merry Christmas though there is not much to feel merry about, to give us the faith to believe that life is not humdrum existence, but is capable of unbelievable wonder, and in the stable that is the human heart, to know God Himself may make His appearance.

Angel With a Broken Wing

The snow—one of those snows where each flake was so big you could not believe in it—should have made it seem like Christmas Eve. But it did not. Perhaps this was because it was twilight. In the city, twilight is a time of day—or is it night?—when it is neither dark nor light, a kind of limbo-ment when the world is not spewed out or swallowed up. This is especially so in winter, when the street lights never seem to be turned on early enough and objects melt into a gray obscurity.

The twilight alone, or the snow alone, would have made for unreality. Together they turned the city into a shapeless, timeless world where everything definite, familiar, usual, dependable was swept away.

It was almost as if God had gone to His window, looked out, and drawn the curtains, but had not yet turned on the lights.

Through this vague void of snow and twilight walked a boy. It did not matter to the boy that every familiar aspect of the street had disappeared; he knew the street as much by his muscles as by sight or sound. He walked up and down it every day, usually several times a day, and he ran up and down it many times more. He lived on the street—in the middle of the next block—and he was on his way home. To get there he simply followed his feet, and they followed each other in a pattern they had learned perfectly, the way a pianist's fingers have learned to pick out a piece of music on a keyboard.

The boy always let his feet take him up and down the street. That way he could let his mind take him somewhere else. And usually it did.

While he was walking down the street, he was also finding his way across an impassable desert, climbing an unclimbable mountain, winning the 5000-meter run at the Olympics or the 500-mile Memorial Day grind at Indianapolis, running the length of the field for a touchdown in the Super Bowl, hitting a home run in the World Series.

Today, in the snow, he was

beating up his brothers. This was a favorite pastime—in his mind, that is. In the flesh, they usually beat him up. They were older, bigger, and stronger.

It was always him against them. At least that is the way it seemed to him.

His brothers were not only bigger and stronger, but different—and alike in their difference. They played together, exchanged thoughts together, and often ran off together and left him. So he tried to come at them unawares; he would pounce on them unexpectedly, trip them when they were not looking, leap on their backs.

This usually brought him a pummeling. It brought his father's wrath down on him too. The boy was very proud of his father. His father was a jet pilot in the Air Force. But he did not think his father was very proud of him.

When his father came upon them fighting, he was the one his father grabbed and swatted. "Leave them alone," his father would say to him. "I've told you a thousand times."

His father never swatted his brothers. They were perfect—like his father. Perfectly big, perfectly

The twilight alone, or the snow alone, would have made for unreality. Together they turned the city into a shapeless, timeless world where everything definite, familiar, usual, dependable was swept away. It was almost as if God had gone to His window, looked out, and drawn the curtains, but had not yet turned on the lights.

Christmas

strong, perfectly smart—perfectly unlike him.

He often heard his father bragging about them to friends.

"Quentin has never made any grade but A," he would say. Or, "Evan has such a high IQ his teachers say he is in the genius class."

When his father was talking to friends about *him*, he was usually saying, "I don't know what gets into that boy!"

At least, that is the way it seemed to him.

He was not big. He was not strong. He was not smart. He did not like school. Not because it was hard; it was easy. But it was dull. He would rather watch TV, or read a book, or dream, or think, or play by himself. When he was not dogging his brothers, he played by himself. His favorite playthings were marbles. He had two cigar boxes full of them. He never played the game of marbles, but for hours playing with the marbles on the rug, he ran sports events, fought battles, dueled, held parades, and organized revolutions.

This Christmas Eve he was walking home after playing football with his brothers. Having kicked off his tennis shoes, he had played in his stocking feet,

and when he put his shoes back on, they were full of snow; but he had played on, shaking with cold, bedraggled, his clothes soaking wet, his teeth chattering until his older brother had ordered him to go home. In reply he had jumped on his brother's back and had been hurled into the snow.

While his older brother held him, his other brother twisted his arm until he promised he would go home. Then they let him up and immediately ran away, shouting what they would do to him if he did not keep his promise.

So as he walked down the street, he was beating up his brothers in his mind.

By the time he reached the street corner nearest his house, he had mentally reduced them to the condition where they came crawling on their knees to beg him for mercy.

And just at this point, unexpectedly, his fantasy changed. Someone in one of the houses along the street must have opened a door, for out upon the air poured the sound of a Christmas carol; it was only a few notes—whoever opened the door must have shut it immediately—but suddenly the boy, almost to his consternation, instead of kicking his brothers as

256

they knelt, was holding out his hands to them—and in his hands were gifts. In one hand he held two Indian chiefs made out of lead, and in the other a penknife. The remarkable thing about these gifts was that of all the things he owned, he esteemed these most. The Indians were a gift from his father. He had many lead Indians, but these two were special; you had only to glance at them to see that they were superior. His brother Evan had always wanted them and had tried to trade him out of them.

His father had given the knife to him, too, and like the Indians it was superior. It contained two blades, a punch, a screwdriver, a can opener, a bottle opener, and a nail file. "That's a fine German knife," his father had told him. "The best in the world!" Not even his older brother had such a knife, and Quentin had wanted it very much.

Now, just as he was about to step off the curb, he paused in his mind and instead of beating his brothers, held out to them these two possessions that were dearest to him in this world.

For a moment, the deep attachment that he felt for his brothers, the fierce longing to be one with

them, came welling up in him so overwhelmingly that it brought him to a halt, half-suspended on the curbstone.

As he paused, through the snow and semidark a car came spinning. Out of control, it made a complete circle and slid sideways directly toward him. A wheel smashed into the curb where he stood; the car bounced, skidded, tipped, righted itself, shot back into the street, and hurtled past.

The boy had involuntarily thrown up his arms. The car was so close he felt it touch a hand, but it merely brushed against his fingers lightly, like a wing, and flashed away.

Everything happened so quickly that the boy had had time neither to move nor speak. Now, as the car disappeared, he waved his fists and shouted after it: "You crazy nut! You crazy nut!"

Then he stood shaking and muttering, not certain whether he was more frightened or outraged.

"You crazy nut!" he shouted once more. But the car had vanished as quickly as it had materialized. The twilight snow filled everything in every direction; even the marks the car had made in the street were already beginning to be obliterated.

The boy started across the street again. But this time, first he looked both ways.

This is how he happened to see it.

Something was lying in the middle of the intersection. The boy ran toward it. It's a woman, he thought. That crazy nut hit her!

Then he stopped short.

It was not a woman.

It was not easy to see just what it was, but he clearly saw bare feet sticking out from under a white robe and then he saw … wings.

Wings! The thing had wings! It's a spaceman, he thought. For a moment he considered running. But only for a moment. If it *was* a spaceman, it was unconscious. Slowly he walked nearer to it. And suddenly he knew what it was. He had seen many pictures—and it was exactly like the pictures.

This was an angel.

The only thing surprising about it was its size. It was huge!

A white robe with a strange fringe hung loosely over the massive body. The boy's eyes took in the bare feet and legs, the burly arms, the huge hands, the gentle face—the eyes were closed—the tousled curly hair, but it was none of these that he really looked at. He looked at the wings. Though he had never seen anyone as big and powerful looking as this angel, not even in a pro football game on TV, he had seen big and powerful men. But he had never, never at all, seen anyone with wings.

The wings were great white feathered things. One of them lay folded at its side, but the other was twisted almost at right angles to the angel's body.

The boy could see in a moment why the angel lay there.

The angel had a broken wing.

His first impulse was to run home for help, but then he realized he could not just leave the angel lying in the middle of the street in the snow.

He looked around, but he saw no one else.

"Help! Help!" he shouted, but no answer came.

It was clearly up to him to get the angel out of the street. Almost without thinking, he reached under the angel's shoulders and with all his power, heaved the huge form from the ground—and almost fell over. The angel came up in his arms as if it weighed nothing at all. *The angel weighed nothing at all!* The boy ran with him to the sidewalk and stood for a moment holding in his arms this great lolling burden that weighed nothing at all. As he carried it down the street toward his house, he kept looking at it in astonishment.

The figure was huge. It sprawled out of his arms. And it was solidly firm. The boy had once shaken hands with Muhammad Ali, but he had never felt such a sense of sheer muscular power as he felt now. Yet the angel was weightless.

It worried the boy, too, that the angel was so big that its broken wing, which hung askew, kept dragging in the street and bumping against things; for from time to time the angel winced, though it did not regain consciousness.

When he got the door of his house open, the boy paused. "Hey!" he called. "Hey!" There was no one home. He carried the angel to his own room and laid it down on his bed. It overflowed the bed. Then carefully, oh so carefully, he lifted the broken wing and placed it in the position that he felt it should have. As he did so, he felt a vast, almost electrical surge that caused his fingers to tingle and his body to glow, but the angel did not move.

The boy sat and watched it. After a while, he became aware that he still had on his wet clothes. He did not feel cold at all. This

This is how he happened to see it. Something was lying in the middle of the intersection. The boy ran toward it. It's a woman, he thought. That crazy nut hit her! Then he stopped short. It was not a woman. It was not easy to see just what it was, but he clearly saw bare feet sticking out from under a white robe and then he saw … wings.

Wings! The thing had wings! It's a spaceman, he thought.

was strange, because he had been shivering before he met the angel and usually just being alone in the house made him feel lonely and cold, even when he was warm. Now, even when he was cold, he felt warm. He pulled off his soaking tennis shoes and socks, went into the bathroom for a towel, came back, and began to put on dry clothes.

He had just finished dressing when he had a sense that he was being watched. He looked at the angel. The angel had opened its eyes—or were they eyes? They were looking right at him, right into him, right through him, but they were the most extraordinary eyes he had ever seen. They were not eyes. They were stars. When he looked at them, it was as though he were looking right through space into worlds beyond his own, worlds of light. The light danced and flickered and shone like flame, for it was the light of stars. He could not say what color the eyes were. At times it was like looking into a day sky and at times it was like looking into a night sky. But always it was like looking through infinites of space, not at eyes but stars. He felt dazzled but at the same time he felt drawn—and he felt peace.

"Thank you," said the angel, "for helping me."

Like its eyes, the angel's voice was strange. The boy was not sure whether the angel spoke or sang. It made the boy think of a choir singing in church on a sunny morning, yet it seemed like speech. Later, when he tried to remember, he was unsure whether he had heard words or thought them.

"A car ran over you," said the boy.

"No," said the angel.

"It almost ran over me," said the boy.

"Yes," said the angel.

The boy and the angel looked at each other.

"Would you like a drink of water?" said the boy.

The angel shook its head.

"A peanut butter sandwich?" said the boy.

"No," said the angel.

The angel reached up and with a grimace pulled its wing more firmly into place. It sighed.

"I—I didn't know what to do about the wing," said the boy. "I hope I didn't hurt you."

"You did beautifully," said the angel. "The wing will be all right. We angels mend fast. A few hours and I will be like new."

"I never thought angels...."

The boy stopped.

"Angels usually do not have accidents," said the angel, completing his thought. "It was clumsy of me. Too little visibility and too much speed."

The boy thought he heard bells tinkling—many bells, gold and silver and bronze and crystal bells. Then he realized he was hearing the angel laughing.

The angel shut its eyes and lay still. When it opened them again, it said, "Your name is …?"

"Johnnie," said the boy. "Do you have a name?"

"Of course," said the angel. "You can call me Mort."

"Mort? That doesn't sound like an angel's name."

"Oh, but it is. A very old one," said the angel.

The boy laughed. "Hi, Mort!"

"Hi, Johnnie," said the angel.

"I wish my brothers were here," said the boy. "Wait'll they see you."

"Oh, yes, your brothers—you were playing with them just before you found me," said the angel.

"Yeah, football."

"Oh, I thought you had been beating them up," said the angel.

"Beating them up?" said the boy.

"You had them crawling on

The angel had opened its eyes—or were they eyes? They were looking right at him, right into him, right through him, but they were the most extraordinary eyes he had ever seen. They were not eyes. **They were stars.**

their knees, as I remember," said the angel.

"Oh, that was only in my mind," said the boy.

"Only in your mind?" said the angel.

"Sure. I didn't really beat them up—I just wanted to," he said.

"That's better?" said the angel.

The boy felt a sudden stab of fear. "Look, if you came because I'd like to beat my brothers up, they're always beating me up. What about that?"

The angel did not answer.

"You think I don't like my brothers, don't you? Is that why you're here?" The thought shot through the boy's mind that tomorrow was Christmas. Perhaps God was checking up on him.

"No," said the angel. "I am here because you *do* like them. In fact, you love them. That is how I broke my wing. At the last moment, my feet caught in your love."

The boy laughed. "Your feet caught in my love? That's a funny thing."

"Love is a very real thing—as you can see." The angel looked wryly at his wing. "We angels are always falling over love—or hate. Just like people."

The boy looked at him as if he did not quite understand.

"But to return to your brothers," the angel went on, "you had beaten them soundly. They were on their knees."

"I'd given them my karate chop," said the boy.

"You know karate?" said the angel.

"Sure. Judo, too; I watch TV."

"But having driven them to their knees, you stopped beating them," said the angel.

"Maybe," said the boy.

"Yes, you held out your hands to them, not in anger, but offering gifts."

The boy said nothing.

"Two Indians and a penknife," said the angel.

The boy ran to the bureau, opened a drawer, and brought out a small box. From it he took two Indians and a penknife and held them out to the angel.

"I see you keep them in a very special place. Do you have other things in the box?"

"Nah. Just personal things."

"Like?" persisted the angel.

The boy looked embarrassed. Finally, he drew out a small, dog-eared snapshot. It was of his father, his mother, and his two brothers, much younger than they now were; he himself was not in it.

"And that's all?"

The boy drew forth a battered earring.

The angel looked at it. "It must be precious!"

"Nah. Just a plain old earring."

"Then why do you keep it? Because it was your mother's?"

The boy looked at the angel almost angrily. "If you know everything, what are you asking me for?"

"Forgive me," said the angel. "I should not pry into your private mind. But it is a habit with us angels." The angel had been examining the Indians and the knife. "I see why you like these so much. They are beautiful."

"The best!" said the boy.

"And you were going to give them away!"

"Not really."

"Tomorrow is Christmas. What Christmas presents they would make! Your brothers would love them," said the angel.

"Huh! What'll they give me?" snorted the boy. "Something from the dime store?"

"Do they have things you would like?" asked the angel.

"I'll say. Lots of things. Lots more things than I have. But they never let me touch them," said the boy.

"For instance?" said the angel.

For a moment the boy's eyes gleamed.

"Quent has a baseball autographed by all the St. Louis Cardinals. It was in the World Series."

"That would certainly be a valuable ball," said the angel. "He probably would not give it to you. Still, your knife and Indians would make beautiful Christmas presents—unexpected ones too. Those are the best kind, are they not?"

The boy laid his possessions on the table and said, "You'd like me to give these to them, wouldn't you?"

"I would like you to do what you would like to do. That is all," said the angel.

"Do you give things to people?" said the boy.

"Sometimes," said the angel.

"I suppose when you want to give somebody something, you just make a wish and there it is—just like that," said the boy.

"Sometimes," said the angel.

"You really can?" said the boy.

The angel nodded its head.

"Could you for me?" said the boy.

"What would you like me to do?" said the angel.

"Get me that baseball."

The boy had no sooner spoken

the words than he held a baseball in his hand. He turned it over.

"Do you really want your brother's baseball?" said the angel.

The boy stood gazing at the ball. Then he looked at the angel. Then he looked at the ball. Then his face clouded with indecision. And a strange thing happened to the ball. The ball began to disappear, not all at once as it had come, but pulsing into view and out again; then slowly, almost as if reluctantly, it vanished.

"It's gone!" the boy exclaimed.

"You wished it to go," said the angel.

"You really can work magic." The boy looked admiringly at the angel. "You made Quent's old ball appear and disappear just like that. I bet you could make this whole house disappear."

"Please do not wish that," said the angel. "We would be out in the snow. You would not be comfortable."

"I bet you could make the whole world disappear," said the boy.

"I will not be called on to do that tonight, I hope," said the angel.

"I bet you could make anything you wanted to happen!"

"There are limits," said the angel.

"If I wanted something else besides Quent's old ball, could you give me that?" said the boy.

"Perhaps," said the angel.

"Could you give me anything I wanted?" said the boy.

"I cannot grant every wish, if that is what you mean," said the angel.

"What kind can't you?" asked the boy.

"I cannot make a person do something he would not do. I cannot keep him from doing something he would do. But I can help him to keep from doing what he does not want to do, and I can help him to do what he wants to do—even when he does not know what he wants. Do you have a wish?"

The boy thought about this for a while. Then he said, "I guess I don't truly know what I wish for."

Just then there was a noise in the doorway. His brothers were standing there. "What are you talking to yourself about?" said Quentin.

The boy looked at his brothers. He looked at the angel. His eyes went back and forth between them. "Aren't you surprised?" he said at last.

"Surprised?" said Quentin.

The boy pointed at the angel.

"At him!"

The brothers looked where he pointed. "Him? Who?" said Evan.

"The angel!"

"What did you say?" said Quentin.

"The angel with the broken wing!"

Quentin and Evan drew back. "Angel with a broken wing?"

"Sure. There in the bed," said the boy.

His brothers' eyes flicked toward the bed, then back at him.

"Don't they see you?" the boy asked the angel.

"Is he nuts?" Evan said.

Quentin winked at Evan. "It's another one of those crazy games he's always playing in his head. You know. Soldiers. Or knights. Now it's angels." Then he looked at the bed.

"Sure I see him. I see him, and I'm going to catch him before he gets away." Suddenly, quickly, he dived toward the bed.

But for once his small brother was even quicker. As Quentin lunged, the smaller boy ducked under him and rising, caught him with one shoulder to catapult him like a projectile. Quentin sprawled on the floor. Red-faced, he rose to his hands and knees. "The rug slipped," he said.

"Do you really want your brother's baseball?" said the angel. The boy stood gazing at the ball. Then he looked at the angel. Then he looked at the ball. Then his face clouded with indecision. And a strange thing happened to the ball. The ball began to disappear, not all at once as it had come, but pulsing into view and out again; then slowly, almost as if reluctantly, **it vanished.**

The boy turned toward the angel. "Don't they see you?"

"I should have warned you," said the angel. "Hardly anyone ever does."

"Say something to them," said the boy.

"I do not think they are in a mood to listen," said the angel.

"Sure he says something to us," said Quentin. "He says you are a nut." Then he nodded at Evan.

The two propelled themselves from opposite sides onto their brother. But just as they flung themselves together, the small boy slipped from beneath their grasp and they crashed into each other, their heads colliding with a loud thump. Both let out a cry of pain and dropped to the floor. For a few moments neither tried to rise. They sat rubbing their heads where knots were beginning to form. At last Quentin hissed at Evan, "Why didn't you watch where you were going?"

Then their father's voice came up the stairwell. "Come to dinner, boys." Johnnie had not known his father was home.

Quentin got back onto his feet. He was still holding his head and staring angrily at everybody—Evan, Johnnie, and the bed. "You've played these crazy

games so long," he said at last. "You're crazy. You think you see an angel with a broken wing. I see a brother with a broken brain. You get that? You've got a broken brain." He rubbed his own head. "And you're gonna have worse than that. C'mon, Evan." The two boys left the room.

Johnnie looked at the angel with dismay and doubt, but the latter merely said, "You do know judo."

"Was that judo?" asked the boy, still breathing hard.

"A perfect performance," said the angel.

"I think you helped," said the boy.

"I guided a little, perhaps," said the angel. "But the truth is they did it to themselves, a case of force reaching beyond itself."

"They didn't see you," said the boy.

"No," said the angel.

"But my dad—he'll see you!"

"He probably will not," said the angel. "I would not advise telling him yet."

"You aren't just in my mind, are you?" said the boy.

"What is just in your mind? What is out of your mind?" asked the angel.

The boy sat and knitted

his brows, wrestling with his thoughts.

"I am as real," said the angel, "as anything in this room. As real as Quentin or Evan. As real as you. Is that real enough?"

The boy did not answer.

"Come here," said the angel.

The boy walked to the bed.

"Take my hand," said the angel, and grasped the boy's hand in his own. Again the boy had that sense of indescribable firmness and strength he had had when he carried the angel. The hand was nothing, nothing at all. Yet the boy knew that he had taken hold of the most real thing he had ever felt. It was so real it made him feel more real—stronger and firmer inside himself.

"You had better go eat your dinner," said the angel.

After dinner, his father turned to him.

"Your brothers have been telling me you have an angel in your room."

The boy looked at his brothers. They were grinning.

The boy said nothing.

"Well?" said his father.

"How would they know?" said the boy.

"Yes, how would they? Did you see him, boys?"

"No," said Evan. "Johnnie said he's there."

"Did you tell them there's an angel in your room?" asked the father.

Johnnie nodded.

"This is a game, of course," said his father.

The boy said nothing.

"Well?"

Still the boy said nothing.

"I guess we should go see." His father took him by the hand and started toward his room. Quentin and Evan started after them. "You can stay, boys," said their father. The brothers stopped.

The angel was still lying on the bed. The boy thought he was asleep.

"Now just where is this angel?" asked the father.

"You don't see him?" asked the boy sadly.

"I certainly don't," said the father.

"He said you probably wouldn't." The boy pointed to the bed.

"In the bed, is he? Let's see." The father walked toward the bed and was about to thrust his hands into the bedclothes when suddenly he choked and began to cough. He straightened, struggling for breath, but the coughing fit would not stop. The boy ran to

267

Quentin got back onto his feet. He was still holding his head and staring angrily at everybody—Evan, Johnnie, and the bed. "You've played these crazy games so long," he said at last.

"You're crazy. You think you see an angel with a broken wing. I see a brother with a broken brain. You get that?"

the bathroom and returned with a glass of water. The father sat down in the chair and drank it slowly. At last he could breathe freely again. He looked at the bed thoughtfully.

"Come here, son," he said, and took the boy on his knees.

"Now how did this angel get here?"

The boy told him how the car had come skidding out of the snow, brushed against him, and hurtled on, and when he had looked up, there the angel lay in the street, with a broken wing.

"You carried him home?" said his father.

"Yes. It's the funniest thing. He's big, but he doesn't weigh anything at all."

"Of course not," said his father. "Wouldn't this indicate he isn't really there?"

"But he *is* there," said the boy, turning to the angel. "Mort, can't you let him see?" The angel only smiled.

"Mort?" said his father. "What is Mort?"

"Mort is his name," said the boy.

"You named him that?"

"No, no. He told me his name," said the boy.

The father stared at the boy and drew him closer. He looked

again at the bed, more sharply and apprehensively than before.

"You're a very imaginative boy," he said. "But it's time now to stop this."

The boy said nothing.

"You are making it up!"

The boy said nothing.

"Look! Nobody but you can see this angel."

The boy said nothing.

"Nobody but you can hear this angel."

The boy looked at his father. His father was frowning and beginning to look angry. The boy looked at the angel. The angel was smiling and continuing to look peaceful.

"Mort!" cried the boy suddenly.

The father rose from the chair and seized him by the shoulder, "Stop it!"

"Mort, Mort!" the boy cried again. "Speak to him. Let him see you, please."

The father shook the boy hard. "There is no angel, do you understand? No angel!" He was shouting. "If you have to play games, can't you play a happy game? Tomorrow is Christmas."

"But it is a happy game," said the boy. "Mort is a very happy angel."

The father gripped the boy's shoulder so tightly that it hurt.

"There is no angel."

The boy shook his head.

"You are not to speak of him again," commanded his father. "This is a direct order."

But the boy continued shaking his head. "There is an angel, there is an angel."

His father raised his hand. But before he could bring it down, the angel reached out its hand and touched him on the shoulder joint. Immediately the arm stiffened and fell rigid at his side. His father grasped it with his other hand and began to rub it wildly.

"What's the matter?" said the boy.

"My arm has a terrible cramp," said the man, his face contorted. Then, suddenly, the arm was normal again. The man heaved a great sigh. Still rubbing his arm, he walked to the door. He stared for a moment at the bed. "I'll be back," he said in a fierce voice and went out.

"You hurt him," the boy said to the angel.

"He felt the touch of a reality beyond his power to bear, that is all," said the angel. "And not for long. I could touch him only because he really did not want to strike you."

"He seemed to want to," said the boy, his eyes full of tears.

"But he did not want to, any more than you wanted me to hurt him. You were angry with me when I did."

"I just wish they could see you. Then things would be different. Why can't they see you?"

"You see me," said the angel.

"Won't they ever see you?" persisted the boy.

"Someday."

"All of them?"

"All of them."

"Will you stay here till they do?" asked the boy.

"My wing will be healed by morning. I shall go then," said the angel.

"I'll be sorry to see you go," said the boy.

"Will you?" said the angel. "I am afraid I have just complicated things for you with your family. And here it is Christmas."

"I know," said the boy. "Do you have Christmas?"

"Every day," said the angel.

"Christmas every day! That must be great."

"It keeps us busy. There is a great deal to do," said the angel.

"Do you get presents?"

"Continually," said the angel.

"And give them too."

Suddenly the boy glanced at the Indians and the penknife that still lay on the table by the bed. He took out two pieces of paper and slowly printed: "For Quentin." "For Evan." One piece he wrapped around the Indians, and the other around the knife, and fastened them with rubber bands.

"I'm going to give them to them," he said.

"I thought you would," said the angel. "You probably will not get the ball, you know."

"That's all right," said the boy. "They're my brothers."

"So they are." The angel looked at the boy for a long time, a look filled with affection and admiration and apprehension. "All human beings are looking for a way to be brothers, do you know that?"

"Yes, I know," said the boy.

"Perhaps you are the one to work out the way," said the angel.

"Me?" said the boy.

"Somebody has to. Why should it not be you?" said the angel.

"It's very important, isn't it?" said the boy.

"The most important thing in the world."

"Like winning a war?"

"It *is* winning the war," said the

"But he *is* there," said the boy, turning to the angel. "Mort, can't you let him see?" The angel only smiled.

"Mort?" said his father. "What is Mort?"

"Mort is his name," said the boy.

"You named him that?"

"No, no. He told me his name," said the boy. The father stared at the boy and drew him closer. He looked again at the bed, more sharply and apprehensively than before.

"You're a very imaginative boy," he said. "But it's time now to stop this."

angel. "Every other war will be lost if you lose this one—even if you win them. Every other war will be won if you win this one—even if you lose them. Do you understand what I am saying?"

"Not exactly," said the boy. "But you mean you want me to try and be a brother to my brothers."

"Yes, and to show others how," said the angel.

"I don't know how," said the boy.

"You did it," said the angel, pointing to the two little packages.

"Yes," said the boy, "but I'm not sure how. It was like working a puzzle and you don't know how you worked it. You just did it. Then you have to figure out how."

"You did it; you can do it

again," said the angel. "It will be even easier next time. And you will get it clear, all worked out."

"I don't know," said the boy. "That might take a long time."

"It might," said the angel.

"I'd better go down and slip these presents under the Christmas tree," said the boy, "so they'll be there in the morning."

When he came back, the angel was sitting on the edge of the bed, so he sat down in the chair. The angel's starry eyes were flashing, and the boy felt himself drawn into them and wandering through their depths. His head began to nod.

Suddenly he sat up. "If I fall asleep, you won't just leave without waking me, will you?"

"We had better say good-bye now," said the angel. "My strength has almost returned."

"Will you ever come back?" asked the boy.

"I will be back."

"Soon?"

"I will be back. If you ever want me enough, you have a wish I have not granted. Never be afraid to wish."

"I'll remember," said the boy. Again his head began to nod. Once he jerked himself awake. Then his head fell forward again.

"Good night," said the angel in a voice so soft it seemed almost the whisper of the snow falling outside the window, only it had a warm sound.

But the boy was asleep.

The angel lifted him gently from the chair and laid him in the bed. It drew the covers over him and for a long time sat watching him. The hours raced toward morning.

Then the father was standing in the doorway, looking into the room. He saw the boy asleep in the bed and sighed with relief. The boy was in the bed; that meant it had been a game; there was no angel. He tiptoed to the bed and adjusted the bedcovers.

But as he bent over his sleeping son, his apprehension returned, for his sense of a presence in the room began to grow again. It was the same sense he sometimes had had in combat—when he felt an enemy plane before he saw it.

Then he looked up and saw the angel clearly. It was standing looking out the window. As the father looked at the angel, the angel turned and looked at the father.

The angel did not say anything, but the stars that were its eyes shone brilliantly, and the man knew that he was gazing into unfathomable depths.

"I felt you knew I was here," said the angel.

"I didn't. Not at first," said the father. "Since you touched my arm, I have been trying not to believe in you."

"I was sure you would see me," said the angel. "You are a soldier, are you not?"

"A bomber pilot, yes."

"You are a lot like Johnnie," said the angel.

"I suppose so," said the father.

"Is that why you whip him sometimes?" asked the angel. "And not the others?"

"I—I don't know."

"We are close. You and I," said the angel. "You thought if you acted certain, Johnnie would begin to disbelieve in me." The angel looked gently at the sleeping boy.

"Do not awaken him," said the father quickly. "He must not know I saw you."

"He will not awaken," said the angel.

A sudden look of fright crossed the father's face.

"I do not mean he will *never* awaken," said the angel quickly. "You know who I am, of course."

"Of course," said the father. "As you say, I'm a soldier. And that name you gave Johnnie. It could

The angel looked at the boy for a long time, a look filled with affection and admiration and apprehension. "All human beings are looking for a way to be brothers, do you know that?"

"Yes, I know," said the boy.

"Perhaps you are the one to work out the way," said the angel.

only be one angel."

"I thought you would recognize it."

"*Mort*. The French word for death. Of course, I recognized it. And why should I not know you? You took my wife."

"Yes. I remember. When Johnnie was born." The angel shut its eyes, and it was suddenly as if all the lights went out. The stars were there, but now they were dark. And the man was staring into dark worlds of mysteries, too deep for him to plumb and understand. Then the angel opened his eyes, and again the room was filled with soft light.

"Why did you come here?" said the father.

"I was on an errand," said the angel.

"The usual one?" said the father.

"The usual one," said the angel.

"To take someone back with you?" said the father.

The angel nodded.

"Johnnie?" said the father.

The angel fixed his eyes with the father's and again nodded.

The father began to walk rapidly back and forth in the little room. He gazed at his sleeping son. Then he stepped quickly between his son and the angel.

"You can't. He's just a boy," he said.

"Sometimes I have to take boys," said the angel.

"But why?"

"Not even I know that. I am the servant of a higher wisdom. It is in charge."

"Take me instead," cried the father in a hoarse voice.

"Such substitutions are hardly ever approved. The rules are pretty strict about that sort of thing," said the angel.

"But it would make sense," said the father.

"To you, perhaps. But there is a higher sense, a divine reason. It is this that runs the world. Its meaning is not always clear—even to me—but it is there. And it is order."

The father still stood between the angel and his son, half-defiant, half-pleading.

"You love him," said the angel.

"Of course," said the father.

"So much that you would take his place and go with me?"

The man looked at the angel as if he were horrified that it could have any other notion.

"Yet you would have whipped him."

The father said nothing.

"On Christmas Eve," said the angel.

"Yes."

"Because he insisted he saw an angel."

"Yes."

"That you saw too."

"I hadn't seen you then."

"All right. That you felt might be there."

The man nodded.

"But why? Why?"

"Because I love him."

"Impossible. And yet, of course. You were bewildered. Frightened.

So you did the thing you have learned to do. You struck out. It is as when you are leading a squadron. The enemy is nearby. You do not know where. But you know what to do: stay in formation! Johnnie had gotten out of formation. You had to get him back."

"I suppose it's like that," said the father. "I knew Johnnie was in danger. And I did the only thing I knew to do. I applied discipline. Force. I did not know what was wrong, but I knew something was wrong."

Then the father was standing in the doorway, looking into the room. He saw the boy asleep in the bed and sighed with relief. The boy was in the bed; that meant it had been a game; there was no angel. He tiptoed to the bed and adjusted the bedcovers. But as he bent over his sleeping son, his apprehension returned, for **his sense of a presence in the room began to grow again.** It was the same sense he sometimes had had in combat—when he felt an enemy plane before he saw it.

"Wrong?" said the angel. "Perhaps it was right. Perhaps it was the rightest thing that ever has happened in your life."

"Right or wrong, I knew something was happening that threatened the way things were—and I had to fight to preserve that way."

"Why?"

The man looked at the angel in surprise and indignation. "Because I'm the father."

"Father, you can be at ease then," said the angel. "You no longer have to guard your son from me."

"But you said you had come to take him."

"I came to take him, but he changed my mind."

"Changed your mind?"

"Yes. The order I serve is not an autocratic one. My Sovereign is no dictator. I, like all my fellows, serve the highest possible purpose, and the wisdom I serve is always love, however you may view it. We angels are committed to obey the cause of wisdom, but we are free. We can follow another course, if something happens that would indicate another course to be wiser."

"And something happened?" said the father.

"I fell and broke my wing!

That does not happen often."

"I've been wondering about that," said the father. "How could an angel break his wing?"

"I ran into an unexpected object—a thought."

"A thought?"

"A thought of love. Johnnie's," said the angel. "As I came down, Johnnie was thinking. It was a small boy's thought of love—but a small boy's thought of love can be unusual—do you not know that?"

"I know," said the father.

"That afternoon Johnnie had been playing football with his brothers. As usual, they had won. So Johnnie had gone off by himself and hated them for a while.

"He told you how he stepped off the curb and the car came speeding around the corner through the snow and half-light. It was just then that he had this thought. He had this thought, and it stopped him, there on the curb, one foot off, one foot on. The car skidded past him, and I ran hard into his thought and it broke my wing."

"What was the thought like?" asked the father.

"That I cannot say exactly. It was vague. Unformed. Unfinished. That is the best word. Unfinished. If he had had it sharp, I could tell

> The father still stood between the angel and his son, half-defiant, half-pleading. "You love him," said the angel. "Of course," said the father. "So much that **you would take his place and go with me?**"

you what it was. Then you could have it, and I could take Johnnie. It was full of love—and power. So loving and powerful that it prompted him to give his brothers two lead Indians and a penknife."

"His most precious possessions!" exclaimed the father.

"He has put them under the tree," said the angel.

The father swallowed hard.

"But the thought that made him do it was not worked out in detail. A small boy's fantasy—little more. Only a step, you understand?"

The father nodded.

"We cannot afford to overlook the least step. It is too important. Humans have to learn how to love. They want to, but they have to learn how. So just on the chance that Johnnie may help them learn how, I have to give him the time."

"You mean Johnnie may be the one to show human beings how to live together?" said the father.

"I do not know. That depends on Johnnie. Somebody is going to."

"But Johnnie!"

"Why not Johnnie? Is he not your son?"

The man looked surprised, as though this thought had not occurred to him.

"Everybody is somebody's son—or daughter," said the angel. "The President. The man who invented the atom bomb. Why not the man who learns to control it? The Man whose birthday you are celebrating today was the son of a carpenter and born in a manger."

The father looked at his son, who stirred in his sleep and smiled. Head tossed back, smiling, one arm thrown out of the covers, he lay sleeping. He is the most completely natural, normal-looking boy I've ever seen, thought the father.

"So he is," said the angel, answering his thought. "Are we not fortunate!"

The father walked to the window. "It's almost dawn."

"Yes, and my wing is mended," said the angel. "Angels never suffer long, though sometimes the hurt is very deep."

"You suffer!" exclaimed the father. "It never occurred to me you might suffer. You have caused so many tears."

"Then would you have me never weep? We angels do not weep often, but when we do, our tears are fire and fall through space. That is one way worlds are formed. On these worlds that once were the tears of angels, life finds its meaning through tears—tears of anguish and tears of longing and tears of compassion. But the meaning that it finds is never a little one."

Is he trying to tell me the Earth is such a world? thought the father; but he did not ask.

"This is Christmas morning," said the angel at last. "Christmas is a family time. My wing is whole. It is time for me to leave."

"Aren't you going to say good-bye to Johnnie?"

"I have said good-bye," said the angel. "He will remember, but he will remember the way we remember all the most important things—as if they were dreams."

The angel stepped to the bedside. He put his hand on Johnnie's forehead, and the boy's breathing became so still the father could not be sure he breathed at all.

"Dream," said the angel to the sleeping boy. "Great dreams! In a moment your sleep will end, but your dreams will not end. They will have only begun."

Suddenly, the starry eyes of the angel overflowed and one tear ran down its cheek, but it did not fall through space and form a world. It fell on the boy's forehead. A soft flame flew up and filled the room with light.

The father felt the light and the flame and with it an overwhelming sense of suffering and longing and compassion, and he felt that all the pain and hope and love that God had felt from the beginning of time was in that room. He uttered a strange cry, and tears began to flow from his own eyes.

"This will never do," said the angel. "It is Christmas and your family has a right to see you happy. Here, dry your eyes."

The angel held out the fringe of its robe.

Before he could think, the father had pressed it to his eyes. The moment he did it, he felt a strange joy—the pain and hope and love were not less, but altogether they formed a joy, an overreaching joy compounded out of them, the way a perfume is compounded out of elements that in themselves are not fragrant.

"Good-bye," said the angel. It looked at the boy and smiled. "I've left him a Christmas present, something for a little boy."

Suddenly where the angel stood, there was an explosion of light that flowed outward to fill the room and then rushed backward upon itself and disappeared into itself, draining all the light out of the room. The father felt

We angels do not weep often, but when we do, our tears are fire and fall through space. That is one way worlds are formed. On these worlds that once were the tears of angels, life finds its meaning through tears—tears of anguish and tears of longing and tears of compassion. But the meaning that it finds is never a little one.

something brush his cheek, and he had the sense of a wing tip, unimaginably soft and unbelievably powerful. He stared at the spot where the angel had been, and he felt that he was staring into an endless and impossible abyss that drew world upon world into it and yet was empty.

Then everything was exactly as it had been before yesterday, except that now it was today.

The boy sat upright in bed, looking wildly around the room.

"Where is he? Where is he?" he cried. His eyes focused on his father. "Dad, it's you."

"Yes, it's me." He walked to the side of the bed.

"But he's gone!" said the boy.

"Is he?" said the father.

"I—I've been asleep," said the boy.

"You have been asleep," said the father.

"Dreaming?"

"Dreaming!"

Then the eyes of both of them were drawn to what the boy held in his hands. For in his hands he held an angel.

It was perfect, the bare feet, the fringed robe, the powerful body, the tousled head, the gentle face, even the eyes that were not eyes but stars. It was a perfect angel,

perfect in every detail—except one wing was broken. It hung twisted by its side.

"It's him," said the boy.

"It's him," said the father.

Just then there came a great shout from the hall and a sound of running feet.

"It's Christmas. It's Christmas. Get up. Get up, everybody! Last one down's a baboon." It was Evan shouting.

The boy looked at his father. The father looked at his son. They reached out, their hands touched, and they went down to the living room. The others were already around the tree.

"Merry Christmas! Merry Christmas!" they shouted.

"What's that Johnnie has?" said his brother Evan. "Why, it's his angel. Let's see that," and he reached out to take it from his hands.

"No," said the father. "It's Johnnie's."

"No," said the boy, "it's not mine; it's ours. It's our Christmas angel. Lift me up, Dad!" He held out his arms to his father. "To the top of the tree!"

With his father holding him, he fastened the angel to the top of the tree.

For a moment they all stood and gazed at it. The room filled with a strange soft light, a little like love, a little like hope, and a little like suffering, yet altogether a joyous light.

But I do not think anyone there saw anything unusual about the light in the room. If they thought of it at all, they just thought of it as the light of Christmas morning, for their own thoughts were full of light.

Then, with a whoop, they fell to opening their presents.

The father felt something brush his cheek, and he had the sense of a wing tip, unimaginably soft and unbelievably powerful. He stared at the spot where the angel had been, and he felt that he was staring into an endless and impossible abyss that drew world upon world into it and yet was empty.

XIV.

Eternity

I am afraid I have run about as far as I can run in the race I am running now. Do not misjudge me. I shall run as long as I can run, and I shall run with all my heart and all my mind and all my might. But … I think I will run a better race if I can rest awhile and renew my strength before I have to run anew.

The Traveler

He has put on invisibility.
Dear Lord, I cannot see—
but this I know, although the road ascends
and passes from my sight,
that there will be no night;
that You will take him gently by the hand
and lead him on
along the road of life that never ends,
and he will find it is not death but dawn.
I do not doubt that You are there as here,
and You will hold him dear.

Our life did not begin with birth,
it is not of the Earth;
and this that we call death, it is no more
than the opening and closing of a door—
and in Your house how many rooms must be
beyond this one where we rest momently.

Dear Lord, I thank You for the faith that frees,
the love that knows it cannot lose its own;
the love that, looking through the shadows, sees
that You and he and I are ever one!

What Lies Beyond?

Beyond the farthest cape, what lies?
Beyond the islands of surmise,
the shallow waters where we ply
our lives, beyond the reach of eye
or even thought, what lies out there?
Sometimes I stand for hours and stare
out, out beyond imagining.
The waves that break around me bring
only a sense of more, yet more.
I think there is no farthest shore.
O God, where shall the limits be?
Your pattern is infinity.

Homecoming

I love this world. You can't write poetry the way I have and not love the world. I'm so aware of its beauty—this windy, watery, blue-green globe I live on! It's a beautiful place and I love it deeply. But I feel that, dear as it is, it's only an inn, only my present place of sojourning. I came here, and at last I'll travel on.

Is there anyone who's never driven down a road and suddenly the country he was driving through was not the country lying round about him but a strange and different country? Yet for all its suddenness and unexpectedness, not an unexpected country. It's almost as if you somehow came up over the hills that hem round the mind and there, spreading out before you, was the native valley of the soul—warm, dear, shining, bringing always a sense of home-coming, always an intimation of perfection, always a feeling that you are about to go back where you belong, a sense of being for a moment in a world far more real and more familiar than the world of every day. It's always only for a

moment—and in a moment you're driving back in the world of every day. A trick of the mind, you say, and dismiss it. But is every day less a trick of the mind, less a state of awareness? Or are there doors and windows in the mind that once in a while—who knows how or why—we open and find ourselves staring into worlds we knew were there but had for a time forgotten? I know past any doubting that this world where now I find myself is not the country of my origin. Dearly as I love it, I am but an immigrant.

Perhaps that's why I love it so much. All I know is this: I've lived before and I will again. That's all that's important. This is the world I've come up to. And the next world will be the world I've come up to, the world I can exist in and can grasp at my level of awareness.

Life did not begin with birth; we have come through aeons of experience beyond imagining. And here we are. In this! In this delightful, sometimes frightful, aching, delicious world!

You are on your way. Your way may carry you to strange and curious scenes, perhaps. Sooner or later, no doubt it will.

But whether it be a world of green skies and purple seas, of fields that lie on edge and hollow hills, or have no skies or seas or fields or hills at all, if thoughts find form and form becomes like thoughts there—still it will be a world where you will be at home.

It will be your world, a world where you can exist, a world that you can grasp and lay hold of in your mind, and with your heart; a world—I have faith—where you can, as you have here, grow to be more than you have been.

There Is a City

There is a city on a hill,
I see it as if far away;
I have not come there, but I will,
for I have sought it night and day.

A city no more built by hands
than heaven's stars or meadow flowers
or human dreams, and yet it stands
vaulting, like banners its bright towers.

Where is the city on the hill?
I seem forever on the brink
of finding it; some day I will—
that hill is in my heart, I think.

If the Slayer Thinks He Slays

How often human beings hold life cheap—their own as well as that of others. This is a terror-filled as well as a wonder-filled fact.

Many have observed that it is much harder to live than to die. We die easily—and kill easily—sometimes much too easily—almost as if to say, "See how easy it is. There is nothing to fear."

We die for love of country, and from pride, and from disappointment, and for love. We give up our lives before we give up our self-respect, and we give them up to win the respect of others. We give up our lives rather than be false to what we believe to be true.

There is some part of us that knows with Krishna: "If the slayer thinks he slays, or if the slain thinks he is slain, neither of these knows the truth about himself. For the Self is never born and never dies."

Some day we shall know why we die, and when we know all the reasons, we shall see that death is a natural part of life, an incident as birth is an incident. And not a cruel and needless anguish—not anguish at all to the dying, only to the living—but a necessary kindness, man having come no further than he has now come—as kind as sleep, as darkness, as winter, as stillness.

Out of God's infinite mercy, God has made the day and the night and divided them with sleep. Eternity might overwhelm us if we had to face or comprehend it all at once, but we can face it and comprehend it one day at a time, one life at a time. When we have no need of dying, we shall no longer die.

Sailor

By ways I never charted
and hardly wished to go,
I have sailed an unknown course
on a sea too wide to know.

I have drifted lost at times,
not sure where the shore might be;
I have searched through storm-tossed nights
for a light I could not see.

But a Higher Wisdom than my own
has had me in its hand,
and I shall trust that it will bring
me safe at last to land.

I Journey On

I am on an immortal journey, and I have yet more journeying to do.

Through chance and change, by way of worlds forgotten and courses unremembered yet graven in my soul, I came up to here, and from here, by ways unknown yet ways my soul has drawn me to, I journey on.

This is the human condition.

I have risen on innumerable mornings.

I have slept through innumerable nights.

I have journeyed on innumerable journeys.

I have lived in familiar and unfamiliar worlds.

I have had brave and beautiful companions, lovely friends. I shall have them yet again.

I have been weak and strong, wise and unwise.

I have come on much curious knowledge, some remembered, some forgotten.

I have done many deeds, some worthy, some unworthy.

What I am undertaking I am not sure—but somehow I am sure it is an enterprise worthy of my effort.

Where I am going I am not sure—but I am sure it is a destination worthy of myself.

Other Products by James Dillet Freeman

Love Is Strong as Death: Moving Through Grief

These touching, powerful poems tell the story of Jim's deep and loyal love for his wife Katherine and how, together, they lovingly dealt with life, dying, and death.

$14.95, hardcover with dust jacket, 154 pp., #48

The Hilltop Heart: Reflections of a Practical Mystic

Venture to a higher ground and gain the hilltop perspective on some of life's most perplexing mysteries and be amazed at how much lighter your heart becomes.

$11.95, softcover, 233 pp., #28

The Story of Unity

This is a factual and fascinating account of how a courageous American couple, Charles and Myrtle Fillmore, gave the world a new, practical approach to Christianity.

$15.95, hardcover with dust jacket, 274 pp., #107

Angels Sing in Me: The Best of James Dillet Freeman

Enjoy a new sense of enlightenment as you listen to James Dillet Freeman himself recite his best-loved poetry.

$9.95, cassette, #7417

To order, go online or call Customer Service at 1-800-669-0282.

www.unityonline.org

Printed in the U.S.A.

130-10541-2M-5-05 B